WORDPRESS WEBSITES FOR BUSINESS

HOW ANYONE CAN MAXIMIZE
WEBSITE PERFORMANCE
AND RESULTS

MICHAEL CORDOVA

BROUGHT TO YOU BY WILDBLUE PRESS
WWW.WILDBLUEPRESS.COM

Any opinions, statements of fact or fiction, descriptions, dialogue, and citations found in this book were provided by the author and are solely those of the author. The publisher makes no claim as to their veracity or accuracy and assumes no liability for the content.

Wordpress Websites for Business: *How Anyone Can Maximize Website Performance and Results*

Published by:

WILDBLUE PRESS
P.O. Box 102440
Denver, Colorado 80250

Copyright 2017 by Michael Cordova

All rights reserved. No part of this book may be reproduced in any form or by any means without the prior written consent of the Publisher, excepting brief quotes used in reviews.

WILDBLUE PRESS is registered at the U.S. Patent and Trademark Offices.

978-1-942266-79-2 tpb
978-1-942266-80-8 eBook

Cover design by Tatiana Villa, VilaDesign.net
Interior formatting by Elijah Toten, totencreative.com
Editing by Andrea Ferak

PRAISE FOR WORDPRESS WEBSITES FOR BUSINESS

"This book is not just about using Wordpress; it is about how to use it to elevate a company and make sales grow immensely. The author shares his experiences and handles the topic in an informal way that enables readers to connect with his words and understand what he is explaining. He speaks about the common mistakes that can kill a company's online presence. The author also shares five powerful checklists/tools that will assist in building the best website possible."

—Mamta Madhavan

"This book is a great tool to help you discover all of the things needed to make a profitable website. The book gives you many ideas with information on how to follow through, making it now than your typical how-to guide. It's easy to understand with terms familiar to the Internet savvy person and explaining the more in-depth details so everything is crystal clear. I will definitely recommend this to anyone looking to build a site for their business!"

—Melinda Turner

"This outstanding book is full of resources & the information you don't find in most books on building sites using Wordpress, written by a man who has built many sites on this platform. It focuses on all the little bits and pieces to make your site run better and be more effective."

—Janet Perry

"This book crossed my path at the exact time that I needed it. I have been using Wordpress for a number of years on a free blogging basis, but have recently been asked to coordinate, design and build an externally hosted Wordpress-based website for an advocacy group. Wordpress Websites for Business was the ideal solution to my questions. There is something about a book that seems more trustworthy than a variety of random website sources. Wordpress Websites for Business has an informal, website feel to it. Short chapters and an informal, personal writing style contribute to this feeling. The author frequently references his own experiences and his qualifications for writing such a book and links to examples.

Overall, Wordpress Websites for Business is a valuable starting point for those who need guidance through the process of setting up a business (or other, all the points are relatable to a range of website types) website. Everything from the basics to more advanced techniques are fully justified, instructions briefly outlined, and a wide range of examples and linked further reading resources provided."

—Madison Dearnaley

"This book is a great resource full of information and the additional resource you need for creating a Wordpress Website. It is easy to understand and implement."

—S Shaikh

DEDICATED TO LAURI AND INEKE

Thank you for sharing your lives and these times we live together in Colorado.

AND TO MY PARENTS DELFIN AND ANTONIA CORDOVA

Who gave Tina, Carrie and me the opportunities.

OTHER WILDBLUE PRESS BOOKS BY MICHAEL CORDOVA

PRODUCTIVITY TOOLS FOR BUSINESS
57 Proven Online Tools to Recapture the Hours of Your Day

Productivity Tools for Business details
http://wbp.bz/57tools

INFORMATION ABOUT MICHAEL CORDOVA
https://wildbluepress.com/authors/michael-cordova-bio/
http://www.21stsoft.com/about-us/
http://linkedin.com/in/michaelcordova

CONTENTS

FIVE POWERFUL CHECKLISTS, ONLINE TOOLS PROVIDED AS FREE DOWNLOADS FOR
BUYING THIS BOOK   15

WHO CAN GET MAXIMUM BENEFIT FROM READING THIS BOOK?   17

WHY YOU NEED THIS BOOK FOR YOUR BUSINESS   19

MY QUALIFICATIONS   21

(EXTREMELY) SHORT HISTORY OF WEBSITES AND THE INTERNET   24

FORMATION OF W3C - THE WORLD WIDE WEB CONSORTIUM   26

EFFICIENCY IN PRESENTATION - CASCADING STYLE SHEETS (CSS)   26

DATABASE DRIVEN WEBSITE CONTENT - CONTENT MANAGEMENT SYSTEMS (CMS)   27

WORDPRESS.COM VS. WORDPRESS.ORG - ALWAYS PICK THE LATTER FOR BUSINESS   30

THE WEBSITE CONCEPT AND WHAT YOU NEED TO PURCHASE   32

BUY A DOMAIN, A BRAND THAT YOU CAN BE PROUD OF   32

GET A SUPER-FAST HOSTING ACCOUNT   33

Fast Page Load Times Can Mean Thousands of Dollars To Your Company   34

Anatomy of a Highly-Optimized Ferrari Web Server   36

A SECURE CERTIFICATE PROTECTS YOUR SITE VISITORS AND BOOSTS YOUR ORGANIC
SEO RANKINGS   40

The Easy Way: Buy Your Secure Certificate from Your Hosting Company   42

Install Wordpress Plugins To Correct Inevitable https Errors   42

The SEO Benefits of Redirecting from HTTP to HTTPS   43

HOW TO SELECT WORDPRESS PLUGINS AND AVOID PESKY PROBLEMS   43

THE DESIGN OF YOUR WEBSITE   44

Wordpress Themes   45

Important Factors in Selecting a Wordpress Theme   47

Typography – A Competitive Separator   48

The Themes I Recommend   49

Customizing Your Theme   50

IMPORTANT WORDPRESS CAPABILITIES - THE LAY OF THE LAND   51

POSTS VS. PAGES   51

SCREEN OPTIONS AND SECTION LAYOUT   52

PERMALINKS   52

PUBLISHING OPTIONS   53

TRASH AND REVISIONS   53

SIDEBARS	54
PLUGINS AND WIDGETS	55
CRITICAL WORDPRESS INITIAL SETTINGS TO MAXIMIZE SECURITY, EXPOSURE AND SEO	58
IF YOU ARE BUILDING THE SITE ON YOUR FINAL DOMAIN	59
Enable Search Engine Indexing	60
Content Distribution To Rule Google 1st Page	60
Maximize Wordpress' Broadcasting of Your Content	61
Free Plugin to Distribute Your Content to 15 Social Media Sites	63
Free Plugin to Plugin to Distribute to 23 Social Media Sites	64
Publish Your Content to 50 of the Top Social Bookmarking Sites – Premium Paid Service	65
DISABLE INDEXING WHEN BUILDING ON A TEMP DOMAIN OR PAY THE PENALTY	66
INITIAL WORDPRESS PERFORMANCE SETTINGS	66
CREATE A CHILD THEME - WORDPRESS BEST PRACTICE	69
INSTALL YOUR THEME FILES	73
INSTALL THE MAIN THEME BY UPLOADING A ZIP FILE	73
UPLOAD YOUR CHILD THEME AND POSSIBLY MAIN THEME FOLDERS VIA FTP	74
WRITING CONTENT THAT SOLVES YOUR CUSTOMER'S PROBLEMS	77
WHAT CONTENT SHOULD YOU WRITE?	77
POWERFUL AND PROVEN SEARCH ENGINE OPTIMIZATION (SEO) STRATEGIES	80
Approaches on How to Create Content That Ranks At the Top of Google	85
Ahrefs	85
Backlinko	88
Mobile-Dedicated or Mobile Responsive Website?	89
Solution and Success-Driven Keyword Research Strategies	90
The Importance of Long-Tail Keywords, Intent and the Mobile Factor	93
The Best Tools to Find Long-Tail Keywords	94
Use Qualified, Prioritized Keywords to Drive Compelling Content	96
Important Places for Your Wordpress Content	96
DON'T FORGET THE STANDARD WEBSITE PAGES	101
LANDING PAGES CAN EXPLODE YOUR CONVERSION RATES	103
Split-Testing and Multivariate Testing of Your Landing Page Content	105
Third-Party Landing Page Tools	106
A Final Note on Landing Pages	106
CONTENT CURATION ENHANCES YOUR AUTHORITY AND MAKES YOU PRODUCTIVE	107
TOP SEO EXPERTS TO FOLLOW AND CONTENT RESOURCES	109

LOCAL SEO REQUIRES YOU JUMP THROUGH EXTRA HOOPS, BUT THE BENEFITS ARE MANY AND MAKE IT A NO-BRAINER　110

CODE YOUR COMPANY NAME, ADDRESS AND PHONE NUMBER (NAP) IN SEARCH ENGINE RECOGNIZED CODE　112

THE AUTHORITY AND PERSUASIVE POWER OF ONLINE REVIEWS　114

The Benefits of Negative Reviews (Believe it or Not)　117

Warning – Don't Stuff the Ballot Box!　120

PUBLICIZE YOUR COMPANY NAME, ADDRESS AND PHONE NUMBER (NAP) IN CRITICAL CITATION DIRECTORIES　121

Consistent and Accurate Citation Listings Are Imperative　124

Google My Business Listing Is the #1 Account To Claim　125

HOW TO SPEED UP PAGE LOAD TIMES BY MULTIPLES　126

THE RETURN ON INVESTMENT (ROI) OF FAST PAGE LOAD TIMES　127

LET'S TURBO-CHARGE YOUR WEBSITE　128

First Back Everything Up!　128

Baseline Your Site's Page Load Time Performance　129

Online Website Performance Testing Tools　129

IMAGE OPTIMIZATION PLUGINS　130

.HTACCESS OPTIMIZATION SETTINGS　131

Browser Object Caching　132

Expires Header　133

GZip　134

Keep-Alive　135

Entire Code Snippet To Copy and Paste Into Your .htaccess File　135

MAINTAIN A HEALTHY DATABASE　138

Optimize the Wordpress Database Manually Using phpMyAdmin　138

Retrieve Your Password From the Database Using phpMyAdmin　139

Plugin to Optimize and Backup the Wordpress Database Automatically　139

LIMIT THE NUMBER OF POSTS ON BLOGROLL PAGES　140

LIMIT THE SIZE OF EACH BLOGROLL POST　141

DISABLE PINGBACKS, TRACKBACKS AND COMMENTS　141

LIMIT THE NUMBER OF REVISIONS SAVED IN THE DATABASE　142

SET UP A CONTENT DELIVERY NETWORK (CDN), THE FINAL STEP IN WEBSITE OPTIMIZATION　142

Why Optimize Wordpress If You're Going To Use A CDN?　143

TASKS/PLUGINS FOR OPTIMUM AND SAFE WEBSITE PERFORMANCE　145

SETUP WORDPRESS BACKUPS – A SAFETY NET　146

What Must Be Backed Up　147

Utilize Your Hosting Company's System Backups	148
Backup Plugins to Automate Backups	148
Automated Local and Off-Site Cloud Backups	148
A Premium (Paid) Backup Tool	149

SECURITY PLUGINS FOR FREE AND ARMOR-PLATED WORDPRESS INSTALLATIONS 150

KEEP WORDPRESS, PLUGINS AND THEMES UP TO DATE – PLUG THE BIGGEST SECURITY HOLE 152

DELETE UNUSED PLUGINS AND THEMES 152

Tools To Manage Multiple Websites 152

SETTING UP WORDPRESS AS A LEAD GENERATION ENGINE 154

Specialized Landing Pages To Drive Conversions for Your Products/Services 157

Competitive Analysis Tools To Smoke Your Competitors 159

Split Testing Tools to Achieve 50% Conversion Rates 160

3rd Party Landing Page Services That Simplify the CRO Process 161

Effective Calls to Action (CTA) Multiply Conversion Rates 162

Autoresponders Communicate With Your Prospects 164

Simple Wordpress Website Forms with An Autoresponder 166

Optional Redirect To A Different Page After Form Completion 167

CRM/Marketing Automation – The Next Level Up 167

Roll Out the Content That You Have Tested and Proven To Convert the Best 168

THE MOST POWERFUL AND VERSATILE SEO PLUGIN YOU CAN GET - YOAST SEO 170

SITE PERFORMANCE PLUGIN TO SPEED UP PAGE LOAD TIMES 172

ADD PAGE/POST TITLE LINK TO FOOTER AREA 173

ACTIONS TO TAKE/PLUGINS TO INSTALL *JUST BEFORE* SITE LAUNCH 175

GOOGLE SEARCH CONSOLE URL SETTING 175

INSTALL GOOGLE ANALYTICS 176

Customized Dashboards For Tracking Sales, SEO, Mobile, Adwords, Social Media, Affiliate Performance... 177

INSTALL/CONFIGURE PLUGINS - THE WORDPRESS SECRET SAUCE 178

Comment Spam Manager 178

Related Posts Plugin 178

Wordpress Cache Plugin 179

Broken Link Checker 180

Visitor Sitemap 181

Structured Data and Rich Snippet Plugins to Separate You From Your Competition in the SERP 182

SOCIAL MEDIA SHARING PLUGINS 186

REDIRECT ALL OLD WEBSITE PAGES TO NEW PAGES – A CRITICAL TASK 186

SETUP ROBOTS.TXT FILES TO ALLOW CONTENT INDEXING	188
CREATE AND INSTALL A FAVICON AND AN APPLE ICON	189
FOR FUTURE REFERENCE, DOWNLOAD A COPY OF THE ENTIRE OLD WEBSITE AND COPY IT INTO YOURDOMAIN.COM/OLD/	190
FINAL PRE-FLIGHT CHECKLIST	191
TASKS REQUIRED TO LAUNCH WEBSITE	**195**
BACK UP/TRANSFER ALL FILES, RESTORE DATABASE	195
CHANGE ALL URLS IN DATABASE TO NEW URL	195
ENABLE WORDPRESS SITE INDEXING	197
ENABLE SITE INDEXING VIA THE ROBOTS.TXT FILE	197
MANAGE DNS RECORDS (TECHNICAL) - CONNECTING TO THE INTERNET	198
MONITOR THE DNS CHANGES YOU MAKE BELOW	199
IF YOU WANT TO MOVE BOTH YOUR WEBSITE AND YOUR EMAIL MANAGEMENT	199
Nameserver Propagation Delay	200
IF YOU JUST WANT TO MOVE YOUR WEBSITE, NOT YOUR EMAIL MANAGEMENT	201
IF YOU JUST WANT TO MOVE YOUR EMAIL MANAGEMENT, NOT YOUR WEBSITE	201
INTERNET OF THINGS	202
MOVE EXISTING EMAILS FROM ONE SERVER TO ANOTHER USING IMAP	202
Tool To Simplify Moving Your Emails To A New Server	204
***AFTER*-LAUNCH TASKS**	**205**
CREATE THEN REGISTER A GEOSITEMAP WITH GOOGLE	205
REGISTER YOUR SITEMAPS AT GOOGLE SEARCH CONSOLE AND BING WEBMASTER TOOLS	206
FINAL CHECKOUT	**208**
GATHER BROKEN LINKS FROM GOOGLE SEARCH CONSOLE, CORRECT WITH AN .HTACCESS 301 REDIRECT	209
USE ONLINE TOOLS TO SCAN FOR SERIOUS ERRORS BEFORE LIFTOFF	209
SET UP A CONTENT DELIVERY NETWORK (CDN)	211
CREATE SITE DOCUMENTATION	**214**
BOOK RESOURCES	**215**
CONTACT ME - REALLY!	**217**
ACKNOWLEDGEMENTS	**219**
REVIEW THE BOOK	**223**
CALL FOR BUSINESS BOOKS	**225**
DISCLOSURE/DISCLAIMER	**227**

WORDPRESS WEBSITES FOR BUSINESS

All links, resources and tools mentioned in this book are listed on the web page listed in the **BOOK RESOURCES** *section at the end of this book.*

14 | MICHAEL CORDOVA

FIVE POWERFUL CHECKLISTS, ONLINE TOOLS PROVIDED AS FREE DOWNLOADS FOR BUYING THIS BOOK

As gratitude for purchasing this book I am providing you with five separate tools/checklists that will assist you in building the best website possible for your business. They are

1. **Wordpress Websites for Business Resources** – A complete list of every one of the resources I use and mention in this book.

2. **32 Keyword Tools** – 30 free and paid keyword analysis tools used by the pros for ideas and for qualifying keywords to ensure you use the most relevant and valuable keywords for your business.

3. **New Website Inventory Checklist** – This document lists and describes all of the important information you need to assemble to get your website built, like hosting, theme recommendations, a list of the important website pages you have to include in your website, logo and images, association logos, social media links and much more. It also includes shopping cart information requirements and important information about comparison shopping engines, which can have a significant effect on your bottom-line sales results.

4. **Sample Wordpress Website Documentation** – To fully document logins, backups and how to use Wordpress.

5. **Source code discussed in this book** - Microsoft Word has a nasty habit of changing some of the characters you type into a document, so I'm providing you clean code in a text file that you can

use directly on your website. The code in that file includes

A. Schema.org code for your web pages to identify your company's name, address and phone number and other critical information, so search engines will recognize your company and check for it in the important local citation directories.

B. .htaccess code to speed up your web page load times.

C. .htaccess code to do 301 redirects.

D. Header code required in your child theme's style.css file.

E. functions.php code to load your parent theme's style sheet on the back-end to speed up page load times.

F. functions.php code to create a shortcode to load your page/post titles into your footer.

G. Footer area code to load the page/post title into a link in the footer of your pages/posts.

H. config.php Code to set the maximum number of stored revisions for your pages/posts.

I. Recommended robots.txt code for your website.

WHO CAN GET MAXIMUM BENEFIT FROM READING THIS BOOK?

This book is for those who own a business or company and want to make sure that the website you are planning meets your performance expectations and does justice to your brand. You don't want to build a new website that does damage to your brand and results in absolutely no leads or sales. If you want performance out of your website in terms of conversions or sales then this book is for you.

Being entrenched in the world of technology and the Internet, I have read countless books and articles about how to apply technology to solve difficult business problems. One of the most annoying things I see on a regular basis is when someone describes a solution without any details as to how to get it done. They just leave you hanging. This is not one of those books. This book lists details of how to perform everything I discuss and lists the online tools to make it easy and get it done right. I have performed these tasks and solved these problems many, many times, and I have found a lot of tools that work as well as as many that don't work at all. I spare you the grief of using tools that do nothing but waste your time.

This book is not intended as a Wordpress primer. There are many other books and places to get basic Wordpress information. I recommend Wordpress for Dummies because that is the first Wordpress tutorial I bought, and it served me well. I bought the paperback, which I recommend for you as well. It has an index in the back which the eBook doesn't (who knows why), and it is handy to have by your side as a quick reference as you're working on your site. I had a site up within a couple days of receiving the book (a potential client who said they'd hire me if I knew Wordpress). If you have spot problems needing immediate answers then you can find a lot of solutions on YouTube.

This book is not simply task-oriented. It is also very strategic. It requires business decisions to determine whether you want to go the route I recommend. Some are time consuming and some cost more than a $4.00-a-month hosting account. If you do, however, follow through with the recommendations I put forth in this book, then you'll see results like those my companies and customers have experienced.

Note that on several occasions I digress into some very technical stuff and include the code and processes required for optimum performance (hosting server configurations, code for optimizing page load times...) but these technical details fill in the cracks that would otherwise be left agape (thus leaving the topics I discuss incomplete) and are indeed necessary if you want to squeeze the very most out of Wordpress.

I have had customers who have built their website multiple times using different technologies and content management systems only to see their traffic, conversions and sales take a plunge. They were coerced by their developer or designer into using nifty features that swished and swooped onto the screen, and had a lot of flashy in-your-face cool stuff. When the site was up you had to click five times to find the product or feature you were looking for, and the point of it all was lost in the pretty confusion.

So, what *is* the point of it all? Well, that's exactly what most websites get wrong. They put a lot of images and content out there focused on selling their wares instead of *solving the problems of their site visitors.* You need to start with your customers and their problems and needs, not your own products and services. You need to fit your products and services into the solutions your customers are looking for.

You always need to ask the simple question: "Is this working?", and if it isn't then you need to change it. Ask yourself that question, as well as "What about this?", and "What about that?", will this tactic, widget, page or tool work for us? You must continually test all of the options that make sense then go forward with what eventually has proven to bring in the best performance – traffic, conversions and sales. You can get your test results to the hundredths. Continual testing is critical to long-term success, and the tools are available that will allow you to make progress every day.

This book is not just a list of plugins. It explains the reason you want to install and set up Wordpress using the methods detailed within, and those reasons are all based on performance. Doing it wrong can cause your business a lot of problems including Google penalties that can take months to overcome. Having said this, I will recommend many plugins and describe how to set them up optimally when appropriate.

If you have a burning desire to make sure that the next website you build is going to change your business dramatically, then you are the intended audience for this book.

Although this book is very specific in terms of the exact tools to use and tasks to complete, it also provides evergreen strategies and concepts that are valid without regard for time or versions of software.

WHY YOU NEED THIS BOOK FOR YOUR BUSINESS

This isn't a book about how to use Wordpress, it is a book about *how to set Wordpress up to elevate your company above your competitors.* I won't guide you click by click through standard Wordpress tasks. There are plenty of books and YouTube videos to learn Wordpress basics. This is not a click-by-click tutorial on how to install plugins and import media files, but a strategic document that ensures your website and content efforts align with your company's goals and objectives to bring you the greatest advantage over your competitors. It describes how to avoid the most common mistakes and those that aren't so common or written about, but that can kill your company's online presence for many months if done wrong.

I'll take you quickly through a few setup tasks and settings that will maximize the results you get from a new website and ensure you don't lose any value of the content of your existing website (if you have one) that you worked so hard to create.

Critical tasks are covered that go beyond everything I have ever read or seen online, in particular in one place of reference. I don't bring up critical topics then leave you wondering how to implement them. I describe what he topic is, where it fits into your business radar, why it is so important and *exactly what you need to do to incorporate it into your website and business processes.* I give you all the tools and tactics you need to build the website that will bring in leads and sales to your business like you have never had before. I describe how to do it, and I show you how to optimize it so that you improve *every day.*

This book is written in the chronological order in which you'd typically build a website in. If you're building a website now, then I recommend you follow the book in the presented order. If, however, you already have a website and are interested in specific items like content distribution, security or backups then you can go straight to those sections and read them individually.

MY QUALIFICATIONS

Well, I've helped my customers grow their sales immensely. I come at it from a different perspective than most, and it is basically technical. A few of my qualifications

Some Successes:

- I increased a software company customer's sales eight-fold from $500,000 annually to $4,000,000 through my SEO efforts.

- I brought in $300K in extra sales in one month for an HVAC customer.

- I increased the number of leads for one customer five-fold when we launched his new Wordpress website.

- I have achieved greater than 50% conversion rates for the sales and lead generation funnels for multiple customers.

My Background:

- BS in Electrical Engineering.

- I founded my company 21st Century Technologies, Inc. in 1993 as a custom database software company.

- I have written software in more than 50 languages.

- I have been designing and building business websites since the beginning of the World Wide Web. This includes building many custom content management systems for my customers. I did this until I ran across Wordpress, and I never went back.

- For 12 years I designed and built custom database software and imaging systems for the biggest semiconductor and pharmaceutical companies in the world, i.e., Intel, AMD, Lucent Technologies, Applied Materials, Johnson & Johnson, Dupont, Bristol Meyer Squibb, Immunex and many more. For some of these systems I built up to three versions across five years.

- With a Top-Secret Clearance I designed and built custom hardware and software systems for the Missile Warning and Attack Assessment mission of the US Air Force at NORAD for seven years. I worked full-time inside of NORAD for over a year.

- After five weeks of interviews by a team of seven investors of a startup company, they hired me to assist in building their website and to orchestrate the marketing and advertising to start the company in the online world. I developed a product release, search engine optimization and pay-per-click advertising plan and successfully executed it. The company was on it's own two feet, and two of the investors subsequently contacted me to see if I was interested in partnering with them in a new marketing agency. Their backgrounds were in direct marketing, and they were interested in my technical and online experience. We formed Mercury Leads in 2006 and I became the CTO of the company. I have since sold the company to my partner at Mercury Leads.

- After a similar monthlong round of interviews with Pedram Shojai, he hired me to assist in his plan to develop the company http://well.org. He owned the domain and was looking for a technical partner to ensure the systems and websites were aligned with his goals for the company. With time Pedram asked me to be a partner, and I became the CTO of Well. org and remain a shareholder in the company. I worked with Well.org to grow our email list to be over 400K.

- In conversations with Steve Jackson, a New York Times bestselling author and college buddy of mine, we discussed the terrible state of being an author in today's world controlled by a handful of huge publishing companies. The publishing companies were paying authors 10% - 15% of the revenues resulting from sales of their book. The situation was leaving authors in dire straits, especially those who had committed to writing full time as their main form of income. After five years of discussing the possibility of creating a publishing company for authors that will fix this and many other problems authors suffer through Steve and I founded WildBlue Press in 2014 and published our first book that August – BOGEYMAN by Steve Jackson. Jackson and I are still running WildBlue Press today having published more than forty books from twenty-five authors, and we're on track to be publishing four books a month.

To summarize, I specialize in the application of technology to solve business problems, and I have done it for many years at a 100% success rate to include mission-critical systems deployed for the US Air Force at NORAD. All of this had led me to doing a lot of online marketing and pioneering search engine optimization and website lead generation tactics that I describe in this book. When I was looking for a tool to build websites, Wordpress was recommended to me, so I checked it out. I compared it to other content management systems like Drupal and Joomla. I found Wordpress to be far superior in terms of its extensibility, ease of use and its built-in search engine optimization capabilities. I started using Wordpress and have never looked back. It is the only tool I use to build websites.

(EXTREMELY) SHORT HISTORY OF WEBSITES AND THE INTERNET

Since this book is about building websites, it is worth a few moments to describe the history of websites and the Internet. This will give you a real appreciation of what you should be doing as a business, why you should be using Wordpress, what tools/plugins you should use with it and why. When you talk to people like web designers, web developers, marketers, they'll give you their perspective of what will work. You'll hear a lot if you've done your homework. I'm doing the same – with this difference:

1. Everything that you will learn in this book works because I have done it countless times for my clients *and have achieved results way beyond what my clients thought possible.* You can see some of their testimonials at http://www.21stsoft.com/seo-web-design-software-development-testimonials/.

2. You'll learn why using Wordpress and the *most effective plugins* will send your site visitors into your sales funnel pre-conditioned to buy and simplify your online presence. This is not about a list of plugins! It is about understanding how to build a website that converts your visitors into paying customers.

3. Although I build aesthetic websites for my clients that represent them in a positive and appropriate light, *pretty websites are not your goal.* Your goal is to present your company and brand *appropriately* and make sure that people recognize the value in working with you *enough that they engage with you after seeing your messaging.* Ultimately it means that every dollar spent will increase your sales. Aesthetics is only one factor in that effort.

4. Nifty, swishy and swoopy images or content used

to be very popular to catch the attention of people visiting websites, but now *it's in the way* of people trying to determine if you can solve their problem. You need to be present your site visitors with intuitive and direct access to your solution to their problems. And consider this – they are only on your site because they have a problem to solve, and they want the solution now. At a minimum they want to know that you are the person or company that will solve that problem.

Static Websites

I have been building websites since the beginning of the Internet and have used many tools and techniques to build them at the highest quality possible.

In the beginning of the Internet you created static websites by coding in the language named Hypertext Markup Language (HTML). You wrote code that was passed from a web server to a desktop browser that allowed you to see the text and image content. Early websites were just that, text content with occasional images thrown in. These original Internet sites had blinking gif images and generally gaudy presentation.

HTML worked well for what it was designed for, but in the end it had many limitations. Here's an example:

Let's say that you have a website that has fifty pages. Your team is very proud of it because you put all of your best minds into creating the content and design. The boss comes in and says that she has had a few phone calls saying that the text is too small to read. She wants the font changed from Times New Roman to Arial and the font size enlarged from 10 to 12 point.

In those days this effort could take maybe a few weeks of effort considering all of the nooks and crannies where text was placed on the website. You would have to go to every individual page and change the code to affect those changes.

It was ugly.

FORMATION OF W3C - THE WORLD WIDE WEB CONSORTIUM

Things improved with time, and fortunately the changes were intelligent. For one thing the World Wide Web Consortium (W3C) was formed. They brought structure to the whole concept of the online world to include what technologies can be integrated into a web page and how information is presented.

The W3C covered topics like

- The coding languages and their structure that you can use to place content onto web pages.
- The security of the information transferred.
- Support of people with disabilities and the US Section 508 Accessibility Program that ensures that people with disabilities can use your website effectively. It's not a given that disabled people can use your site, and it takes extra efforts and coding to make that happen. For example, if you are building a website meant specifically for US federal employees to learn a program, then it is required by US law that you are Section 508 compliant.
- Efficiency in presentation.

EFFICIENCY IN PRESENTATION - CASCADING STYLE SHEETS (CSS)

So, back to the problem of changing the fifty pages of content so your site visitors can easily read it.

The W3C very intelligently conceived a new language and technology called Cascading Style Sheets (CSS) that changed the game. The invention of CSS allowed you to define a style once, *and immediately deploy it across your entire site!* If you want to change the font type and size then you can change it in your style sheet code once, and it will affect the entire site at once. CSS was a huge advancement in web technologies.

So, of course someone saw the power of CSS technology and took it to the limit. Dave Shea, a developer from Vancouver, Canada, decided that he'd use CSS to *completely* manage a website's design. He built many websites that completely abstracted the aesthetics from the content. By changing the style sheet file the website looked completely different. He published his designs at http://csszengarden.com. The concept caught fire and many other developers contributed their style sheets to present the same content in new and wild designs. When you visit CSSZenGarden.com you'll be fascinated to see that every one of the hundreds of designs actually present the same content, but in a radically different design and context.

DATABASE DRIVEN WEBSITE CONTENT – CONTENT MANAGEMENT SYSTEMS (CMS)

As I built websites for companies, the problem I ran into was that they wanted the content changed. Always. This is, by the way, very normal. I was the logical one to do it since I had built their website. At the time there was no concept of a website content management system. My customers would call me with the changes they wanted and I'd make them. It ended up that they didn't want to pay my development rates for simple website changes. It was a problem because they didn't know how to make the changes themselves because they didn't know HTML or CSS, even though as a part of my services I provided copious amounts of documentation on how to manage their website. What to do?

I started my company 21st Century Technologies in 1993 to design and build custom database software systems for companies that needed to improve their efficiencies and automate their repeatable processes. It was a logical next step to build websites with content that was fed from a database. I consequently built many database-driven websites for my customers. Eventually this became a standard technology called content management systems (CMS). For several years many CMS systems vied for the top of the heap. Ektron, Drupal, Joomla and Wordpress were a few of the mainstream CMS systems. There were many, many more. I tried all of the ones that made sense.

My initial introduction to Wordpress was when a company out of California contacted me to build websites for their customers. They had a corner on the market of building websites for law firms in northern California. I had not used Wordpress before, but they said it was a job requirement since that was their platform of choice and the basis for all of their other websites. This was compelling so I bought Wordpress for Dummies and dove in. I have since determined that Wordpress is the best solution available for building websites that my customers can maintain themselves.

The top three CMS systems in use today are Wordpress, Drupal and Joomla. They are all open source (for the purposes of this discussion this means they are free to download, install and use) and each has a development community that creates themes and plugins allowing you to change your design and add functionality to your website without having to write the code for it yourself. You can Google "wordpress drupal joomla the numbers" and see how they compare with each other. At the time of this writing here is how they stack up

- Wordpress has roughly three times the number of downloads that Joomla and Drupal combined with greater than 140 million downloads.
- Wordpress has twenty times the number of websites

of Joomla and Drupal combined at greater than 75 million websites.

- Wordpress occupies 65% of the CMS market share with Joomla at 13% and Drupal at 8%.
- Wordpress has 3000+ themes with Drupal at 2000+ and Joomla at 1000+.
- Wordpress has 36K+ themes with Drupal at 26K+ and Joomla at 5K+.
- All three can be installed in less than 10 minutes, with Wordpress coming in at 5.

Wordpress started as a blogging tool and is now widely used as a general content management system. It is now *the only tool I use to build websites for my clients.* The main reason I use Wordpress is because it performs. By that I mean it has excellent search engine optimization (SEO) capabilities right out of the box, and I can efficiently create websites that convert visitors into leads and sales for my clients. The Wordpress plugins that you can use for free or for a minimal cost allow you to setup a sales funnel (another big topic in itself) that brings in leads when people complete a form to download your expert white paper or download your digital products. I just checked the results of one of my client's sites, and we are getting a 50.5% on our reservation landing page. That means over half of the people that visit the page fill out the reservation form. Their site generates about 500 reservation requests per month. That doesn't count the phone calls they get which we actively solicit in the site as well. With the average reservation bringing in $1,000 and an average close rate of 33% this is more than $166,000 worth of leads per month coming in from the website. That can sustain and grow a business!

So, Wordpress just works. I'll now get straight to the point of how to setup a website for your company in a way that maximizes your search engine exposure and increases your leads and sales.

WORDPRESS.COM VS. WORDPRESS.ORG – ALWAYS PICK THE LATTER FOR BUSINESS

There are two kinds of Wordpress. They are built from the same core code and have the same *general* capabilities, but one is much better for your business.

- **Wordpress.com** is a hosted platform where all you have to do it create an account, do a little customization then start adding content. You don't need a hosting account because they host your site. For $99/year (at the time of this writing) you have the option of using your own domain, and for three times that price you get access to premium themes and the privilege of using Google Analytics. There are some critical ingredients missing, however, and that is the reason Wordpress.com is not the best tool for use as a company website platform.

- **Wordpress.org** is the option where you need both your own hosting company and domain name. *The Wordpress.org option provides the secret sauce of Wordpress sites – plugins and unlimited themes and customization!* What are plugins you ask? A plugin is a set of code written by someone else that provides functionality that you need, at either no cost at all or at a minor cost to you. You can see the popular free ones listed here: https://wordpress.org/plugins/browse/popular/. Some have over a million installs. You can get plugins for security, image management, editing, page cloning, sliders (images that rotate with options for text, embedded html and animations), image galleries, sitemaps, forms management, image optimization, broken link checkers, events calendar and a lot more. Believe me, unless your needs are very specific to your company, there is a plugin already written for the functionality you need.

It may cost you a few bucks, but it is out there. A few bucks meaning maybe a $25 one time fee. With the Wordpress.org option you have full access to all of your Wordpress files and architecture, so your flexibility is infinite.

What other options exist other than Wordpress and the popular open source platforms mentioned above, you may ask? Well there are sites like Wix, Weebly and Squarespace. They are very popular in that they are platforms that make it very easy to setup a website. Their limitation is that they don't provide the flexibility and access that a Wordpress. org website provides, and *they don't have the capability of adding the powerful plugins or the hundreds of thousands of developers that the Wordpress.org option provides.*

Wordpress.org has the largest development community of any content management system in the world. That means there are a lot of people out there with needs and requirements that write the code that meets their needs, then many of them provide it to the world (usually) for free.

I recommend Wordpress unequivocally to everyone. It is simply the best platform that you can build your website with. When a company wants to hire me to build their website in a platform other than Wordpress, I always decline. I explain that they'll want ease of use and performance (conversions and sales) out of the website, and anything other than Wordpress will not provide them the performance they are looking for. Wordpress will. It is truly the best option for a business website, so if you are still waffling on the platform for your site then end it here and now. Wordpress is what you are looking for.

THE WEBSITE CONCEPT AND WHAT YOU NEED TO PURCHASE

In order to get an appropriate Wordpress website for your business you'll need to purchase the following at a minimum:

- **A domain name** – the ones for my current companies are 21stsoft.com, wildbluepress.com and well.org.
- **Hosting** – this is where your website resides on the Internet. It is ultimately a physical computer that your domain points to.
- **A theme**, the design for your site. I generally use premium themes that come with support and many professional features that I use for my client sites.

BUY A DOMAIN, A BRAND THAT YOU CAN BE PROUD OF

Since your domain name is your brand and part of your company's face to the world, it is important to spend some quality time and conversations considering what it should be. Ideally it would be short, and incorporate the name of your company.

It used to be useful to buy many domains comprised of the keywords that you want your company to be found by in the search engines, then point them all to your website. Those days are over. Not only is this not going to get you that keyword traffic, but your website will be penalized because all of those domains have the same content. This is called duplicate content by the search engines nowadays, so you need to avoid this.

So, think about your domain name then go to GoDaddy and buy it.

Another domain you might want to purchase is a short one to use in social media. Since Twitter limits character count, using short URLs allows you to add more hashtags and content to your tweets. For this purpose I use the domain 21st.bz for my short URLs. Since the name of my company is 21st Century Technologies, Inc., 21st.bz is easily identified with it.

A note about URLs (Uniform Resource Locators). A URL is a website address. The name was obviously created by tech geeks, but all it means is a web page address. These are typical URLs:

http://www.21stsoft.com

http://21st.bz/reviews

Your domain name is part of the URL, but the URL is used by browsers to address a website.

GET A SUPER-FAST HOSTING ACCOUNT

If your company depends on your website for reasons of branding and/or attracting leads or sales, then your responsibility to your company is to make sure that your website always represents you in the best light. That means a lot. If someone arrives at your site thinking of hiring a professional window installation and sales company, and your website has any of these problems, then you're dead, and all of the time you spent building your site has been wasted:

- Bad design
- Inappropriate content
- Difficult to navigate
- Slow page load times

This section is about the page load times. It doesn't mean you just get fast hardware. It means that *all of the software* that runs your server and website are optimized for Wordpress and have the absolutely fastest execution. With the right effort (detailed below) you can drop your page load times from 10 seconds to less than 2 seconds.

It is incumbent on you to provide the best visitor experience, and starting out with fast web servers can make all of the difference.

I recommend SiteGround and Hostgator for their robust servers, support and scalability. Most of my sites and customers are hosted at these two hosting companies. They can grow right along with your business as your hosting needs change. If you want the Ferrari of web hosting, then read on. In the next section I describe how to optimize a managed web server to achieve the ultimate in website page load time performance, so don't jump into a hosting company yet. It costs a lot more, but it is central to your success, so you at least have to consider it.

Fast Page Load Times Can Mean Hundreds of Thousands of Dollars To Your Company

Several years back Google started charging their Adwords pay-per-click customers more dollars per click if their landing pages loaded slowly. This was a costly reality check for companies that were lazy in their landing page design. This showed Google's emphasis on the user experience.

Google soon after rolled out the same concept into their organic rankings. Slower page load times resulted in lower organic rankings.

The message is clear. You need to arm yourself with the tools and techniques that make your website content load lightning-fast, or pay the price. The obvious rewards are better search engine rankings and lower PPC costs. Both of these are important for any company attempting to improve their company's online presence.

According to KissMetrics[1], the business and financial reasons for fast load times are compelling:

- A one-second delay in page load time decreases customer satisfaction by about 16%.

- 44% of online shoppers will tell their friends about a bad experience online.

- 52% of online shoppers state that quick page loading is important to their site loyalty.

- 40% abandon a website that takes more than three seconds to load.

- 79% of shoppers who are dissatisfied with website performance are less likely to buy from the same site again.

- *A one-second delay in page response can result in a 7% reduction in conversions.*

So, page load time is important, and it goes directly to your bottom line.

Two examples with dollar figures to consider:

If your site is making you $100,000 per month then you're losing $84,000/year if your site experiences a one-second delay. Multiply that by eight to $672,000 in the case of a very typical Wordpress ten-second page load time to two seconds. You can see what fast page load times can do for your company. Not to mention the improvement in visitor experience and satisfaction. Test your page load time at http://www.webpagetest.org/ to see where your site is currently at and what the possibilities for improvement are.

This is an analysis I recently sent to a client of mine:

At fifteen leads/day and each one worth $500, thirty days of leads (450 leads/month) is worth $225,000.

---

[1] Sean Work, "How Loading Time Affects Your Bottom Line", https://blog.kissmetrics.com/loading-time/

The home page currently takes 5.8 seconds to load according to webpagetest.org.

Taking the last number from the list above (7% loss of conversions for every second a page takes to load), if we removed four seconds from the page load time we can possibly increase the number of conversions by 28% from 450/month to 576/month with an increased value of those leads of $63,000 with a total monthly value of the leads of $288,000, up from $225,000.

The benefit is $63,000/month, and the monthly cost for this is $220/month for hosting with all of the features that I recommend putting into the server.

We're talking more than two orders of magnitude in financial benefit each month, and you'll also have many happy website visitors because they don't have to wait forever for pages to load.

For details on how to speed up your page load times, see the HOW TO SPEED UP PAGE LOAD TIMES BY MULTIPLES section below.

Anatomy of a Highly-Optimized Ferrari Web Server

The following is an excerpt of my post at Quora: https://www.quora.com/Which-hosting-is-good-to-host-WordPress-And-how-to-install-WordPress/answer/Michael-Cordova-1.

The diagram below shows you the communication of an optimized request/response cycle between a browser and a web server when someone browses to a web page. It is complicated, but it can be optimized. The gray boxes are the components that will speed up your pages immensely. They are all explained in the diagram below.

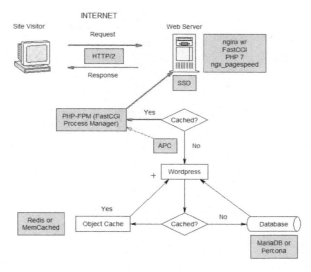

HTTP/2 - allows for an unlimited number of requests per connection between a browser and a web server. HTTP/1 is extremely inefficient requiring multiple requests to serve web page content.

nginx - pronounced engine-x, is web-server software. For years Apache was the web server of choice, but the performance improvements in nginx have moved it to the top for hosting websites on Linux servers.

FastCGI - runs PHP as a separate service from the web server software instead of weighing down the web server software allowing for a better efficiency.

PHP 7 - currently the latest version of PHP.

ngx_pagespeed - minimizes css and javascript. This removes unnecessary whitespace which can amount to a great deal in the size of the files, and improves page load times.

Solid State Drive (SSD) - instead of a spinning disk to hold a computer's data, an SSD is electronic memory used as a hard drive. It can improve a computers data access speeds by a factor of two to five times that of a regular hard drive.

PHP-FPM (FastCGI Process Manager) - executes PHP code outside of the web server thus reducing server load. It also allows APC cache to be shared across multiple processes which saves memory (potentially an order of magnitude when combined with nginx) which provides scalability and allows for more processes and traffic.

reverse proxy - manages secure SSL communications.

APC - Alternative PHP Cache is an opcode caching plugin for PHP that avoids executing PHP scripts by executing pre-compiled code if the same script has already been executed.

Redis or Memcached - both perform persistent object caching. If you have a distributed architecture, then Redis is your tool, otherwise Memcached is a simpler device that stores database or REST API queries.

MariaDB or Percona databases - latest versions of the MySQL database most commonly used with Wordpress.

So, setting up a Linux server for fast page load times is a significant technical feat. Unless you are a Linux administrator I suggest you have your hosting company take care of it. I Googled managed VPS hosting and contacted twelve companies. The managed part is important in that they'd do the server configurations discussed in this section for you. Some have multiple levels of managed hosting. *You absolutely need to do your own due diligence!*

Your hosting company may provide quick Wordpress install software like Softaculous, but if they don't then you can use the famous five minute manual install. Just go to Wordpress. org and click the download button on the home page. You have to create a database at your hosting company and connect it to your Wordpress installation, but the effort is fairly painless. I'm not detailing this process here because most hosting companies, and the ones I recommend above offer simple and automatic Wordpress installs that will only take you a couple minutes.

I'm obviously very serious about site performance. I have spent a lot of time on this subject and created the diagram above as an explainer for my clients, so they understand the benefits and value of maybe a $150-$300/month expense. The dollars mentioned above that you can capture by having a site that loads in a second or so easily justify the cost and effort of moving to optimized hosting if your site is intended to bring in business leads or sales, and your company depends on it. Two of my clients currently have load times of 1.6 seconds. That's snappy. One of them gets about 400 leads a month that are worth $500 each for a monthly value of their leads of $200,000! For a meager $250/month expense they stand to capture hundreds of thousands of dollars per year in extra revenue by optimizing their web servers and page load times.

My Top-End Hosting Recommendation

If you need highly optimized web hosting and fast page load times for Wordpress then I heartily recommend (drum roll please)...

Managed Hosting by Rose Hosting

Their responses to my pre-sales inquiries and their costs for the features I required drove me to go with them for my own companies and for my customers. Their expert advice and their knowledge of server configurations and optimizations after I hosted with them are better than I have ever worked with. *The page load times are now at 1.6 seconds!* Because of this, I highly recommend managed hosting from Rose Hosting.

A SECURE CERTIFICATE PROTECTS YOUR SITE VISITORS AND BOOSTS YOUR ORGANIC SEO RANKINGS

An important feature to have on your website nowadays is a secure certificate. It encrypts communications between a visitor's browser and your website server. It is important for privacy reasons, and it is now a Google ranking factor as well. It uses https instead of http and the "s" part implies usage of the Secure Sockets Layer (SSL) of the http protocol that is used to transfer web page content from a browser to a web server and back.

There are multiple types of certificates:

- Basic certificates that encrypt your main domain only.

- Wildcard certificates allowing you to secure subdomains as well as your main domain. For example, if you have created a separate mobile site like https://m.yourdomain.com (which I recommend that you do), then you can encrypt that subdomain also.

- Enhanced warranties - in case your site is compromised then you are insured for more against losses. These are typically used for high-ended eCommerce sites. A basic certificate insures you for maybe $10,000, and the enhanced warranty can insure you for $1,750,000.

The SEO factor: In August of 2014 Google announced that having an SSL certificate on your website will improve your organic rankings. With time they have said that it is being weighted even more than it was originally. In the case of *your rankings*, it can be the tie breaker between your site and another when all other ranking factors are equal, and yours has an SSL certificate and theirs doesn't. It may put you on the first page of the search engine results pages instead of the second. It may put you into the second position instead of the third, or the first instead of the second which could make a real difference in the traffic to your site.

According to a Chikita report[2], the first position gets 32% of the traffic, the second gets roughly half that and the third gets about half of the second. One notch up in your rankings can help you in a big way, and installing an SSL certificate may just be the answer to getting it done.

The process of installing a secure certificate on your web server is somewhat of a technical feat. In short, this is the process:

1. Export a Certificate Signing Request (CSR) and private key from your web server. This is a block of text that is needed by your Certificate Authority (CA). A CA is a company like Symantec, Thawte or Comodo.

2. Purchase a secure certificate from a CA, and give them the CSR and private key.

3. Your CA issues a secure certificate which is another big block of text.

4. The secure certificate text file must then be submitted to your web server, and from that point forward all references to your website can use https instead of http, and the communications will be encrypted.

I have performed manual secure certificate installations as explained above several times. I don't recommend it. If you do decide to install a secure certificate manually, then *make sure to note the date of expiration on your calendar!* They are in yearly increments. I'd buy at least a two-year certificate. If you don't do this then the certificate will expire, all https references to it will fail and your site will go down. Not pretty, and not fun to deal with.

---

2   The Value of Google Result Positioning, https://chitika.com/google-positioning-value, (June 12, 2013)

The Easy Way: Buy Your Secure Certificate from Your Hosting Company

I suggest buying a secure certificate from your website hosting company and putting it on automatic renewal. If and when there are problems they'll take care of it. You should still put the expiration date on your calendar, maybe a week before it expires, then contact them before it expires to verify what will happen when the expiration date arrives.

Install Wordpress Plugins To Correct Inevitable https Errors

In the Installing Wordpress and Initial Settings section below I recommend that you set your Wordpress URLs to https://yourdomain.com. Even though you now have a secure certificate and the URLs are set to use https, you can get SSL errors due to using third-party, external resources like social media icons from other plugins. SSL errors like this will pop up security warnings in forms and erode the confidence of your site visitors, so you need to correct this problem.

I use a these five plugins to fix this. Try them starting from the top as different ones work based on your unique installation:

- Cloudflare Flexible SSL (assuming you have set up Cloudflare)
- Really Simple SSL - this plugin alone can possibly fix the problem
- Fix SSL/Non-SSL Links
- SSL Insecure Content Fixer
- WordPress Force HTTPS

In general they'll make sure that all objects on the page use the secure https reference instead of non-secure http to load the page objects. They cover all of the bases needed to ensure all objects use https to access the page. If one doesn't work then add the others one at a time. Start with the default settings and adjust as needed if you get https errors after installing them. For the Cloudflare settings you'll have to contact their tech support directly.

If your SSL is setup correctly, you'll see a lock image *without a triangle warning icon* next to the left-end of your website addresses like this:

If there are errors in your https setup then you'll see a yellow warning triangle in front of the lock. If this happens then you'll need to dig into the settings of the five plugins mentioned above.

The SEO Benefits of Redirecting from HTTP to HTTPS

If you don't redirect from http to https then both versions of your pages will exist. Performing a 301 (permanent) redirect from http to https for all site pages forces only the SSL version of the page to exist as far as SEO is concerned. This combines the SEO ranking juice for both versions of the page and boosts the SEO value of it.

HOW TO SELECT WORDPRESS PLUGINS AND AVOID PESKY PROBLEMS

Before I talk any more about plugins, I want to discuss how to select plugins in a safe manner that minimizes risk and potential problems.

To find and install plugins, you typically log into Wordpress, click to Plugins > Add New, then type in a search term like "social." You'll see all of the plugins listed that Wordpress determines to have met your criteria in relevance order. They are each listed with their number of installs, their average five-star rating and the total number of ratings.

Before you install any of them (!), and in order to qualify each plugin you're considering, first click on the More Details link below the Install Now button. Carefully note each of these items for each plugin:

- Last Updated – if it was last updated years ago then Click the X icon at the top-right and move on. Wordpress changes too often for a plugin that is this old to be considered reliable.
- Average Rating and number of ratings – Good and many are obviously best.
- Number of active installs – there is a big difference in the stability of a plugin that has 25 installs vs. one that has 100,000+.
- This mention at the top:

If this warning pops up then you obviously need to reconsider using that plugin. If the plugin was last updated recently, has hundreds of thousands of installs and many ratings with an average of four+ stars, then you might consider ignoring the warning and installing it anyway.

When selecting a plugin for any particular purpose, it is important to select a reputable plugin and developer. If a plugin has a pro version then it lends more credibility to the developer in the sense that they are more committed to keeping their plugin up-to-date. Check out their pro version to see if their premium features are what you're looking for, and if so then consider buying it. They are usually pretty cheap.

Using these guidelines will minimize your plugin woes.

THE DESIGN OF YOUR WEBSITE

The design of your website should generally follow its purpose. As Louis Sullivan said:

Form (ever) follows function

The look and feel as well as the websites functionality and operation would typically stem from the type of business you have, and the type of website that would most appropriately serve your business. An eCommerce site would have different content and operate differently than a lead generation site. A photography site would be different than one for an association. The content and usage would be different in each of those cases, so, as you continue into the next section about themes, keep that in mind.

Wordpress Themes

Another one of the major benefits of Wordpress is that you can install one of hundreds of thousands of themes available from countless theme developers. There are many sources of both free and premium themes. It is (usually) the theme that gives your website its looks. I say usually because you can spend many weeks tweaking the look of your website by changing the cascading style sheets and creating custom images to improve the look of your website. Today's themes provide great tools to get the design you want, so going to those ends isn't required. It totally depends on exactly what your own personal preferences are.

Free themes may initially sound enticing, but there are unseen costs associated with using a free theme. When you use a free theme you don't get the high-ended features like ease of customization or dedicated plugins for things like easy sidebar and footer content management. Since a theme is just a set of code, if there are security problems with your free theme then you are on your own as far as getting them corrected. It happens, and this is not a trivial problem to fix. When you purchase a premium theme *and create a child theme from it as described below*, then you can upgrade the theme as the theme developer discovers security issues or improvements. It may cost you something like $50/year to subscribe to the update service, but if you are building a site for your business then this is an incidental cost.

One type of premium theme is one that doesn't require any coding to make detailed design changes such as header colors, background images and font colors. These themes allow you to log into Wordpress and do all of the customizations you want by simply changing settings. I have found that there are still customizations that setting changes don't allow for, so I always recommend creating a child theme regardless of the theme capabilities. Make all of the setting changes that you need, and if you don't have the capability to make the final tweaks needed for your intended design then you can go into the style.css and functions.php to make final customizations.

Other advantages of using a premium theme are

- They come with support. You will have problems and it is always good to have a safety net where you can ask questions and get answers from a competent support team. You don't have to get too far into your website and development effort before questions come up, and having capable technical help will ensure you get the website that you want.

- They keep up with security and Wordpress updates.

- They keep up with the latest standards and SEO requirements such as making the theme mobile-responsive. *This is not trivial.* This is code that is included in your style.css and functions.php files that is as technical as it gets. If your site isn't mobile-responsive then you're basically dead as far as the search engines go. You don't want to be coding mobile standards into your theme yourself unless you are an experienced developer. Mobile responsive is also an important SEO factor.

- They are usually optimized for page load times, which, as discussed above is an important usability and SEO factor.

Important Factors in Selecting a Wordpress Theme

I have written a comprehensive blog post about the important considerations of picking a Wordpress theme. I'll list the highlights here, but you can read the full post at: http://www.21stsoft.com/how-to-pick-a-wordpress-theme-quickly-to-save-time-and-money/

Here are the basics of selecting a viable Wordpress theme for your business:

- Perform an analysis of your competitors to make sure you don't miss important or critical features that would place you behind them if you miss these features.

- Create the content and images for several of your most important pages and place the content into your posts and pages as you're finalizing the theme layout and aesthetics. Make design tweaks and ensure that the theme will work for these key pages.

- Pick a fast framework that is mobile responsive with flexible layouts and all of the features that you require. Mobile responsive means that the layout of the content changes based on the width of the page, or the device viewing the page. WooCommerce themes are some of the best eCommerce themes available. In May 2015 WooCommerce joined Automattic, the developer of Wordpress itself, so you can be assured that it will always be compatible with Wordpress.

- Use a theme that focuses on the main goals of your website like an eCommerce site, a blog, a lead generation site or a photography site.

- As mentioned above, pick a theme that allows you to manipulate the sites typography *out of the box*. The fact is that you can always integrate any typography into your theme by coding it into your style.css file, but it gets complicated and requires a technical

Wordpress developer. Ideally your theme would support many typography options, so you don't have to do this custom coding. Many modern Wordpress themes have typography features built into them by going to a place like Customize theme > General > Typography.

- Think about integrating your logo and branding before you spend a lot of time on many of the other aspects of the site. It's difficult or time consuming at a minimum to change all of the colors of an entire theme, so at least start with a theme that has colors close to those you require as far as light vs. dark.

Typography – A Competitive Separator

Typography sounds like a term used by professional designers, and it is indeed exactly that. The good news is that, due to today's theme designers recognition of the value of cleanly designed website typography, tools to quickly implement a powerful typography on your own website are readily available to you.

You don't tell people you're funny, you tell them a joke. Similarly, it's one thing to say you're a designer, and another entirely different thing to show it as you can see in Chris Wilhite's home page layout (chriswillhitedesign.com) below.

You need to think about the type of information you want on your website, then how best to display it. White space is important for an uncrowded presentation. It's not always what you say, but how you say it, and typography allows you to portray a sense of consideration of aesthetics instead of (like most websites) just listing pages and pages of text with a few images.

It is worth your time to do the following before you pick a theme (which is described below):

1. Scan the websites of your primary competitors and industry leaders and note the types of fonts used. A serif font is one that has little tails on the letters like times new roman uses. A sans serif font doesn't have those tails. Arial is one of the most widely used sans serif fonts. See how Chris Wilhite uses both types of fonts above.

2. Note the spacing between lines of text. This is the line height.

3. Note the spacing between areas of text and the edges of the box or area that encompasses the text. This is the padding.

With these thoughts in mind, think about who you are, what you want to present and how it can be displayed with an aesthetic appeal that shows your company has taken the time to think through the presentation of your ideas, products and services to express them in visually creative and unique ways.

The Themes I Recommend

Some of the premium Wordpress theme frameworks that I have used and recommend are Elegant Themes, the Genesis framework at Studiopress.com, ThemeForest and WooCommerce. I have used the Divi theme from Elegant Themes a few times, and I'm impressed with its layout capabilities. It has many objects that you can add to your pages that bring a sophistication to your site to separate you from your competitors like styled calls to action, animated buttons, filterable portfolios, countdown timers, sliders and accordions. The main reason I like the Divi theme so much is because it is simple to use and empowers my clients to make beautiful and powerful websites without any technical expertise.

Another Wordpress drag and drop page builder worth mentioning is Beaver Builder. It got rave reviews and an A+ rating in a WP Beginner review of drag and drop page builders for ease of use, flexibility and design output. It is a premium plugin that costs $99 and up, is beginner-friendly and includes inline on-boarding capabilities that make it simple to get started. I use it with the Divi theme on many sites.

Customizing Your Theme

After installing your theme there are many aesthetic and functional changes that you can make, and a standard place to make those changes. Once you are logged into Wordpress go to the menu options Appearance > Customize to make changes that the theme designer allows you to make on your own without coding. It is here where you usually change your logo, color scheme, default page layout and many other options.

Each theme works differently than the others, so the theme you select may have more customization capabilities above and beyond what is described in the paragraph above. For example, Studiopress themes can also be customized in the Genesis > Theme Settings section, and Divi themes can be customized in the Divi > Theme Options and Theme Customizer sections.

IMPORTANT WORDPRESS CAPABILITIES – THE LAY OF THE LAND

Before jumping into Wordpress strategies and setup, I want to give you an idea of some of the important Wordpress features and those that separate Wordpress from the rest of the pack of other content management systems.

Although I do assume you are familiar with the Wordpress basics, these features are so important that I want to make sure you are aware of them.

POSTS VS. PAGES

Out of the box Wordpress has two main types of content that you can publish – posts and pages. The main differences between them are

1. Posts have categories. Think one to three categories per post.

2. Posts have tags. Tags are keyword phrases about your article. To get your content indexed most effectively, you should always add five to fifteen tags that accurately describe the content of the post.

3. When you publish a post, Wordpress pings all of the sites you have listed in your Update Services list (explained below) notifying them that you have just posted new content.

4. Pages have neither tags nor categories, and publishing a page does not result in Wordpress pinging all of your update services, which is one of the reasons that they are referred to as *static* pages.

The significance of categories and tags is that Wordpress automatically creates a separate page for each category and tag. Every post that is tagged with a specific word like *golf clubs* will have a page created for that tag, and all posts that are tagged with *golf clubs* are on that page thus making it highly optimized for that keyword. Same with categories.

So, if your content is important at all, then you probably want to use posts to get maximum exposure and distribution for the content you create in Wordpress. More on the distribution later.

SCREEN OPTIONS AND SECTION LAYOUT

Every screen inside of Wordpress is configurable in terms of what you see and where it is located on the page.

To add or remove sections, scroll to the top of the page and click the Screen Options tab. Then you can check and uncheck the sections to enable them as needed.

To re-arrange where each section is located on the page, just grab the title area, and when the mouse turns into a cross, drag it to the area where you want it, then let go of the mouse to drop it into that area.

PERMALINKS

One of the advantages of Wordpress is that you can create search engine-friendly URLs like this:

http://yourdomain.com/
how-to-make-carne-adovada-tacos

instead of this:

http://yourdomain.com/id=1574

URLs like these will improve your search engine rankings, and the number of clicks to your site because people can see what the article is about before they click on your URL.

To make you URLs search engine-friendly log into your Wordpress site then go to Settings > Permalinks > Common Settings > Post name, then click the Save button.

BONUS Tip: Sometimes, for many possible reasons, your interior pages may not load with the SEO-friendly URL. When this happens just go back into your permalinks settings, change them to the default setting, then back to the Post name setting and save again. This will fix this problem nine times out of ten.

PUBLISHING OPTIONS

When you are done editing a page or a post, you make it live by publishing it. You can either click the Publish button in the Publish box at the top-right and have it go live immediately, or to the right of where it says Publish immediately there is an Edit link. Click that, then you can set a date in the future to have it published automatically on that date and time. This is particularly handy when you have a workflow of creating many posts at once. You can schedule them to be published in the future on any schedule of your choice.

TRASH AND REVISIONS

When you delete a post or a page they are not actually deleted. They go into the Trash bin. You can simply click the Trash link at the top of your posts or pages and restore any post you want. You can also empty the Trash which permanently deletes them.

Every time you edit a post or page and click the Update button Wordpress saves a record in the database of that version. If for some reason you need to rollback to a different version then on the edit page open up the Revision section, select the version you want to roll back to, review it to make sure it is the one you want to restore, then click the Restore

This Revision to restore it. If you don't see the Revisions box then scroll to the top of the page, click Screen Options, check the Revisions box, close the Screen Options then scroll down to the Revisions section.

SIDEBARS

Sidebars exist ideally to support the content on your pages. At my publishing company WildBlue Press we have a unique sidebar for each book title, and a general one that lists our latest releases and news events that goes on pages not specific to a title. For example, the sidebar for LOCKOUT by John J. Nance at https://wildbluepress.com/lockout-john-j-nance-mystery-thriller/ lists the book sales buttons, a radio interview with the author and several of his blog posts about the book.

LOCKOUT, by the way, is an excellent aviation thriller that I highly recommend. Like I said to the author John Nance, it is the first time that I felt like breaking out into applause when I finished the book. It is truly a scintillating and a great read that you won't forget. Nance has sold millions of books, and we at WildBlue Press are very fortunate to be publishing his thrillers.

The sidebar on my 21st Century Technologies, Inc. home page at http://www.21stsoft.com has a widget for my most important and popular content with tabs for Guides/Current Hits/All Time. Widgets like that on your default sidebar serve as a central point to promote your main products and services. Be creative. What are the goals of your website? Create a plan to present your products and services on your most important pages. The home page of your site gets most of the traffic, so keep that in mind when you select the content and sidebars for it. More on widgets in the next section.

Take a step back and think about the sidebars you might want that will support your site content. Three to five sidebars specific to your products and services is typical. Think along the lines of how the entire site content breaks out, and what you might want to have as ancillary content to support the article and main content they're reading, or at least promote your goals like to buy a product or guide them to your main content areas.

If you use the Studiopress Genesis themes, then I recommend that you use their Genesis Simple Sidebars plugin to add the sidebars that you need. The fact that it is created by the theme developers is good insurance that it will be maintained.

If you don't use a Genesis theme, then I recommend using the Free Custom Sidebars plugin by the people at WPMUDEV, the premium developers of Wordpress multi-user plugins and themes. You can get a description of using it at https://premium.wpmudev.org/blog/free-custom-sidebars-plugin/. Using plugins from WPMUDEV is great assurance of the plugin's long-term viability because it is created by a long-term developer of some of the most powerful Wordpress plugins ever envisioned and made available to the public.

PLUGINS AND WIDGETS

One of the most important and powerful features of Wordpress is that it employs an open architecture that allows for easy and simple expansion of the capabilities that Wordpress provides for you out of the box. By installing a plugin you can add features from software *that someone else has written.* Most of the plugins I use on my websites and those of my clients are free. Sometimes you run across plugins that have a professional paid version, and if their features meet your needs, then I suggest purchasing them. The costs for paid plugins is maybe $20 or $50, or a monthly fee of $5 or $10. They don't break the bank.

A plugin is a self-contained piece of software that is installed by going to Plugins > Add New when you're logged into your

Wordpress back-end. This allows you to add all kinds of functionality, including widgets. A widget is an object than can be dragged and dropped onto a sidebar. It is a visual object that performs a special feature. Plugins don't have to include widgets, but other than the widgets that come with Wordpress, installing a plugin is the only way to add new widgets. Plugins can perform functions like security, external updates, backups, etc.

Widgets are managed in the Appearance > Widgets area. Go there and you'll see some boxes on the right side. Click on the down-arrows to open them. Those are the sidebars, or, more descriptively, widget areas. On the left-side of the page are the widgets that you can click and drag into the widget areas on the right-side, then configure them so they appear in the sidebars of your sites pages and posts. Examples of widget uses are

- Features posts that show the title, featured image and an excerpt of, say, a category of posts.

- Popular posts.

- Text widgets that allow you to add text or HTML code to place content like testimonials and images.

- A list of all of your post categories or tags. Many times tags appear in a Tag Cloud. This is a listing of all of your popular tags with the words of the tags varying in size based on the amount of times the tag is used. Bigger fonts for a tag imply that that tag has been used more than the other tags.

- A newsletter signup call-to-action.

- A mobile app download call to action (you have a mobile app don't you?).

Plugins can also run behind the scenes without a visual component like a sidebar widget. In this case they perform functions like:

- Website security

- Backups of your database, themes, plugins and uploads folders
- Spam protection
- Page load time optimization
- Image compression
- Contact forms
- SSL object corrections
- Social media distribution of posts
- Website page caching

CRITICAL WORDPRESS INITIAL SETTINGS TO MAXIMIZE SECURITY, EXPOSURE AND SEO

So you have a domain name, a hosting account and a theme for your website. The next step is to put it all together and get your website up.

Bluehost and many other hosting companies use a set of software called cPanel that provides many capabilities, and all the tools that you need to install and manage your website. To install Wordpress, log into your hosting account and in the cPanel click the Install Wordpress icon. Amazing huh?

All Wordpress installation scripts are different, so the fields of data they ask for varies. In many they create the administrator password and email it to you. If, however, they do ask you for an admin password then *I highly recommend using an extremely difficult password.* Use upper and lower case letters, numbers and many special characters like !@#$%^&*()~+_-. Make it thirty characters or longer in length. Use a difficult username as well. *Never* create a Wordpress installation with usernames like admin, wordpress, your real name or your email. Use usernames like See3Pe!Yo#Twenty16LovesT4RwaR5. Since Wordpress is the biggest kid on the block it is also the most targeted CMS for malicious attacks. Creating difficult usernames and passwords is the first step in thwarting those attacks. Using simple ones all but guarantees that your site will get hacked.

You should use a secure password manager for everything you do online that requires logins. It simplifies logging into any online site and saves your passwords securely. I, personally, have used RoboForm for over eight years, and have used LastPass in the past several years for scenarios where multiple people have to share logins. It has a powerful capability that allows you to allocate login permissions by groups. This is a huge benefit to my companies. Both RoboForm and LastPass are extremely secure and easy to use, and both also have the nifty capability of saving all fields of online forms for future similar forms that you have to fill out repeatedly.

IF YOU ARE BUILDING THE SITE ON YOUR FINAL DOMAIN

An important factor to determine whether you build your website on the final domain or if you build it on a temporary domain is whether there has previously been a website residing on your final domain. A reason for building it on the real domain is because the website is a fresh new one on a domain that hasn't had a website before. If, however, you already have a website on your domain and you're replacing it with a new Wordpress website, then you should build it on a temporary development URL. When you do this you also *must* shut off all indexing and content distribution of your posts. If you don't do this, then as you build your website on the temp URL the search engines will read and index all of it and attribute all of your great content to the temp URL. Then, when you deploy the exact same content on the new website at the final domain, your company's real domain *will get penalized for duplicate content!* It can be very difficult to pull your site out of this penalty box. It can take several months to forever for Google to forgive you of this mistake. The most compelling advice that I have read in forums to correct this penalty was, depending on the severity of the Google penalty, to change your domain name! You don't want to deal with this, so doing it right as explained here is your only option.

In the case of building on your real and final domain you want the search engines to see all of the content that you're adding *as you add it.* This shows them that you are actively working on the site and creating great content. Search engines love that. They'll come to index your site content often to get the latest changes and additions, and they'll give you better rankings assuming you are adding quality content.

Below I explain the details of performing these tasks.

Enable Search Engine Indexing

When you are building your site on a domain that has never had a website before, then you want your content to be seen by the search engines as you build it. You need to change Wordpress settings to allow this. Do so by going to Settings > Reading, *un*-checking the "Discourage search engines from indexing this site," and clicking the Save Changes button.

Content Distribution To Rule Google 1st Page

After you have allowed search engines to consume your content, you want to get maximum exposure for it. Wordpress can distribute your content to many other sites when you publish it, and that's what this section is about.

The subject of content distribution is one that I recommend you commit to for the long-term. I'll give you some guidance here as well as some of the current tools available, but the tools change, so you need to always keep this on your radar. You can distribute your content to all of the top social media sites, RSS feed directories, bookmarking sites as well as ping sites that relay your posts to other sites that are always looking for great content. Plugins are created now and then that automate the process of sending your content to these sites, so you should keep up with this topic so your blog posts will get maximum distribution across the top sites on the Internet.

This topic is even more important today and in the future because social media sites have cut back on your friends and connections that actually see your posts. This goes for Facebook and Twitter as well as most (if not all) of the major social media sites online today. Their usual business reason for this, whether they state it publicly or not, is to boost their advertising. When you advertise on their site your posts get more exposure. By maximally distributing your content to many more sites than just the top social media sites then you simply have more eyes on it. This is important to the long-term success of your website.

There is a lot that you can do for your site's search engine optimization and organic rankings which I'll discuss later in this book, but what I discuss below is low-hanging fruit, costs nothing but a few minutes of your time and always gets you excellent exposure and results.

Many customers have achieved 4, 5 and 6 of the top 10 positions in the search engine results page by following these tactics. My advice is to do the following, then write optimized blog posts that include your main long-tail keywords to splatter your content all over the first page.

Maximize Wordpress' Broadcasting of Your Content

One of the out-of-the-box features of Wordpress is that it has the capability to notify other sites each time you publish a post. It uses an XML-RPC protocol to ping other sites in a format that allows them to grab your content and place it onto their site, or relay it to others. This gets your content in front of thousands of people on authority sites and blogs with a link to your post! This is a huge SEO benefit as well. The better the quality of your content, the better the chances of other sites posting it on theirs, so always make sure to write quality content that is relevant to your customers. Provide solutions and ideas instead of sales pitches.

To notify hundreds of ping sites each time you publish a post in Wordpress, first go to this blog post of mine:

http://www.21stsoft.com/
how-to-massively-distribute-seo-content-in-seconds/

And click the link that says

huge list of 330 tested ping sites

Copy the entire list to your clipboard. Next, in the Wordpress admin paste the list into the Settings > Writing > Update Services box at the bottom of the page and save your changes.

If the Update Services box isn't available then there could be one of a few problems. Here's how to fix them:

1. You aren't allowing search engines to consume your content. In this case go to Settings > Reading > Search Engine Visibility. Is the "Discourage search engines from indexing this site" checkbox checked? If so then you are blocking the distribution of your content. Uncheck it, save, then go to Settings > Writing > Update Services, paste the list into it then save.

2. You are on a Wordpress multi-site installation. By default, editing the Ping Services for a WordPress Multisite network site is disabled. This can be re-enabled with a plugin such as the Activate Update Services plugin.

3. You are on a Wordpress.com site. Wordpress.com sites are not ideal for businesses, so I'd look into getting a hosting company and moving to a Wordpress.org site where you have all of the capabilities you'll need to run your company's website. This is discussed in the Wordpress.com vs. Wordpress.org section above.

By default Wordpress comes with one ping site installed, Ping-O-Matic, "A Wordpress Foundation Contraption." Ping-O-Matic relays your content to fifteen other sites. This list of 330 ping sites will greatly enhance the online exposure for each of your posts as Wordpress will now automatically broadcast your posts to each of those sites.

Free Plugin to Distribute Your Content to 15 Social Media Sites

Pinging your content to hundreds of content sites gets your content out there, but sending the same message to the top social media sites, to your friends that have expressed an explicit support for your company is even more important. These people have Liked your Facebook page and shared your content, followed you and shared your tweets, followed and shared your pictures in Pinterest. They love what you're doing in social media, so you need to send them the blog posts that you spend so much time on.

One free plugin that can accomplish this is Jetpack. Jetpack comes installed with Wordpress by default, and it is created by the Wordpress team. This makes it a preferred plugin. Preferred because you are generally assured that the plugin will always be compatible with the Wordpress version changes. At least you can rely on this more than most plugins created by third parties.

To enable Jetpack you have to connect to a Wordpress.com account because it uses some of the services associated with it. Go to Wordpress.com, create an account then use that same login to connect Jetpack on your site to it. Next you'll enable the features you want to use in Jetpack. I recommend activating all of the following free categories which will enable several more features discussed next:

I won't go into all of the features, but if you want to know more about them you can go to the Jetpack page:

https://wordpress.org/plugins/jetpack/

You can also click on the features in the Settings page to see a description of each of the features. There are many more features than what is shown in the image above. You can see them in Wordpress at Jetpack > Settings. The feature we're interested in for this conversation is Publicize. On the Settings page scroll down to Publicize, run your mouse over it and click the Settings link. There are fifteen social and media sites you can enable. You just need to activate them individually. Once you have done this, each time you publish a post it will be distributed to each of the sites you have authenticated. Here is a list of the sites Jetpack Publicize publishes to:

You can click the "More information on using Publicize" link at the top-left for detailed instructions on using the Publicize feature to the fullest extent.

Free Plugin to Plugin to Distribute to 23 Social Media Sites

Regardless of having said all of the above about Jetpack being written by Wordpress, there is another plugin you might want to consider–Nextscripts: Social Networks Auto-Poster (SNAP). I won't go into a lot of detail on this plugin other than to say that it is another viable plugin free content distribution that you might want to consider. Information about the plugin is here:

http://www.nextscripts.com/social-networks-auto-poster-for-wordpress/

At the time of this writing it is compatible with the latest version of Wordpress, was updated three hours ago, has 100,000+ installs and an average rating of four out of five stars.

Publish Your Content to 50 of the Top Social Media and Bookmarking Sites – Premium Paid Service

The premium service Onlywire at http://onlywire.com publishes your content to fifty sites. It is actually more than that because you can publish to multiple Facebook Pages. Onlywire takes input from your site's RSS feeds and relays it out to the top sites on the Internet.

The time-consuming part of using Onlywire is creating the accounts where your content will be distributed. My suggestion is to go to a virtual assistant site like fiverr.com or seoclerks.com and have it done for you for a few dollars. Give them your new Onlywire account login and have them connect to each of the accounts. This will save you tons of time and cost $5.00 or $10.00. Have them provide you with all of the logins in a spreadsheet then change your Onlywire password when they are done.

One drawback of this service isn't a fault of theirs. It will be the same for any other service that connects to the networks/social media sites. The API connection for some of the media sites times out after thirty to 180 days, so you have to refresh their login inside of Onlywire periodically. If you are committed to maximizing your content's reach, then this is a minor inconvenience.

DISABLE INDEXING IF YOU ARE BUILDING THE SITE ON A TEMP DOMAIN OR PAY THE TOUGH PENALTY

When you are building your site on a temporary development URL, then you want to avoid search engine indexing of the content at that temp location. In this case you already have a website on your target domain, and you're building a new Wordpress site to replace it. This effort ensures that the content created on a temp site is not consumed by the search engines. If you don't take this step then the temp location will get credit for all of the content. Then, when the site goes live on the real domain you'll be penalized for all of the duplicate content. This can hurt you for months *or longer* and potentially squash all of the benefits of creating a new website. I have read forums where people are desperate to get back into Google after a penalty like this. One of the recommended solutions was *to change the company name!* You don't need this.

To stop Wordpress from allowing your content to be indexed at the temp location, go to Settings > Reading, then check the "Discourage search engines from indexing this site" checkbox and click the Save Changes button.

INITIAL WORDPRESS PERFORMANCE SETTINGS

After Wordpress is installed, these are the quick settings that you should make immediately:

I. Go to Settings > General and do the following:

   A. Set the Wordpress Address (URL) and Site Address (URL). I prefer to use a URL without a www, and, assuming you have installed a secure certificate as described above, then the URL for both of these fields would be https://yourdomain.com.

1. Set the timezone and the starting day of the week to Sunday.

2. Go to Settings > Permalinks and set it to Post name. This will yield user and SEO friendly page names like yoursite.com/how-to-install-wordpress/ instead of yoursite.com/?p=777.

3. Go to Settings > Discussion and at the bottom set Avatars > Default Avatar to Gravatar. Logo. This shows comments with the commenter's own picture if they have set one at Gravatar.com.

4. Go to SEO > Titles & Metas > Taxonomies > Categories, then set Meta Robots to noindex and set Yoast SEO Meta Box to Hide. This and the next three settings avoid duplicate content issues.

5. Go to SEO > Titles & Metas > Taxonomies > Tags, then set Meta Robots to noindex and set Yoast SEO Meta Box to Hide.

6. Go to SEO > Titles & Metas > Archives > Author Archives Settings, then set Author Archives to Enabled and set Meta Robots to noindex.

7. Go to SEO > Titles & Metas > Archives > Date Archives Settings, then set Date Archives to Enabled and set Meta Robots to noindex.

The other security measure that you must take is setting up daily and regular backups. By having a good copy of the database and all of your website files you can restore a completely compromised site in minutes. This is detailed below.

Many themes come with a home page configuration where you add all of your home page content into widget areas at Appearance > Widgets. Every time I have used a theme like this it has been very confusing, especially for my clients who will be changing their own content. The layout is pre-set and rigid, and since text widgets don't have a toolbar to manage the rich content, it is very difficult for a nontechnical person to add and edit home page content. For this reason I recommend making the home page a static Wordpress page where you have ultimate flexibility as far as what content is on your home page and how it is displayed.

To use a static page as your home page do the following. Create a page and for now name it Home Page. You can change it later. Then go to Settings > Reading > Front Page Displays. Click A static page, then in the dropdown list for Front page select the Home Page you just created and Save Changes.

Set Your Preferred Website URL

Your website URL preference settings are important for your search engine optimization. There are many ways links can reference your website home page. Here are a few examples:

http://www.yourdomain.com

http://yourdomain.com

http://www.yourdomain.com/index.php

http://www.yourdomain.
com/?campaign=promo_4-2017&state=Nevada

If each of these is used to point to a website in links from other websites, then the SEO value is split across them and consequently the overall SEO value of those links is diluted. Fortunately Wordpress takes care of this problem.

To set your preferred URL in Wordpress go to Settings > General > WordPress Address (URL) and Site Address (URL). Set both to either http://www.yourdomain.com or http://yourdomain.com. This will perform a 301 redirect from the URL with the www to the one without it or vice versa depending on your preference. An http 301 redirect is a permanent redirect from one URL to another, and it passes 90-99% of the SEO juice from one page to the other when you change pages.

CREATE A CHILD THEME - WORDPRESS BEST PRACTICE

This is a techie effort, but makes for a clean and safe installation and sets up your company to allow you to refresh your theme with the latest files when the developer updates it to fix bugs or security issues. It is very typical that you'll want to tweak your theme design, and you don't want to lose those updates when the main theme gets updated. Colors, spacing, fonts, etc. are common changes that you'll make. I have never installed a theme without needing to customize it, sometimes with ever so small tweaks. The problem when you do this to the theme that you installed is that when the theme developer has an update to his theme then it will wipe out your customizations if and when you update his theme. Creating a child theme avoids this problem. The main theme can be updated safely, and you'll keep all of your customizations in a separate theme. The child theme is a theme that sits beside the main theme folder, and uses all of the facilities of the main theme.

Here is how to create a child theme:

1. Start by downloading and unzipping your original or purchased premium theme and placing it into a local folder on your computer like:

\webs\yourdomain\wp-content\themes\themename\.

2. Create a folder at the same level as \themename\ named with a keyword phrase relevant and important to your business like denver photographer. It will look like this:

\webs\domainname\wp-content\themes\
denver-photographer\

The standard Wordpress naming convention for a child theme is themename-child, but I recommend bucking this convention and using your most relevant keyword phrase instead. By doing this you'll be getting SEO mileage from the name of your child theme since that keyword phrase will appear in the content of every page of your site. Make sure the child theme name uses hyphens in place of spaces.

3. Using a code or text file editor, create a file named style.css and place the following code into it:

```
/*
Theme Name: Divi Child theme
Theme URI: http://www.elegantthemes.com/gallery/divi/
Template: Divi
Version: 1.0.0
Description: Smart. Flexible. Beautiful. Divi is the most powerful theme in our collection.
Author: 21st Century Technologies, Inc.
Author URI: http://www.21stsoft.com
Tags: responsive-layout, one-column, two-columns, three-columns, four-columns, left-sidebar, right-sidebar, custom-background, custom-colors, featured-images, full-width-template, post-formats, rtl-language-support, theme-options, threaded-comments, translation-ready
License: GNU General Public License v2
License URI: http://www.gnu.org/licenses/gpl-2.0.html
*/
```

The line with Template: Divi ties your child theme to the original theme, and without it, or if the name of the template theme is misspelled then your child theme won't work, so make sure it is verbatim the same as the original theme name.

4. Create a file named *functions.php* and put the following code into it. It will import the parent theme on the back-end, so it is a lot quicker than using @ import coding in the style.css file on the client-side:

```php
<?php
add_action( 'wp_enqueue_scripts',
'enqueue_parent_styles' );

function enqueue_parent_styles() {
    wp_enqueue_style( 'parent-style',
get_template_directory_uri().'/style.
css' );
}}
```

If you are a php developer, then you'll notice there is no closing php tag in the code above for the *functions.php* file. If it was there then the last line in the file would be:

```php
?>
```

Wordpress *functions.php* files don't end with this standard closing php tag because after the functions.php file is loaded there is more PHP code that executes after it in the sequence of events, so Wordpress doesn't require a closing php tag for this file[3].

5. Create a file named screenshot.png as the theme image that identifies the child theme and is selectable inside of Wordpress. Make it 1200 x 900 pixels and place the new theme name such as Denver Photographer Theme into it, and your

---

3 Chris, The Crimson Coder, "Why do some functions.php file contain closing tags and others don't?", https://premium.wpmudev.org/profile/chris171/, (October 9, 2014)

company name and logo if you so desire, then place it into the same child theme folder:

\webs\domainname\wp-content\themes\ denver-photographer\[4].

This image will be shown when you are logged into Wordpress and are selecting the theme to activate as you'll do in the steps below.

---

4 "Theme Development", https://codex.wordpress.org/Theme_Development

INSTALL YOUR THEME FILES

So, what you have now is two folders that contain all of your theme files. You now need to upload them all to your web server. This doesn't make them live. It simply makes them available as options for your websites theme. To make them live you have to log into your Wordpress account and activate your new child theme.

INSTALL THE MAIN THEME BY UPLOADING A ZIP FILE

In the section just above about creating a Wordpress child theme I suggested unzipping the theme files and placing them into a folder. You can, also, directly upload the zip file they have provided for you. Note that this only holds for the main theme and not the child theme you have created. This section describes how you can upload and install the theme file directly without using an FTP client, which is explained further below.

After you purchase your premium theme, you need to download the zip file containing all of the files they have provided to you for the theme. The zip file that you have to actually install might be inside of that original zip file that you have downloaded (every theme developer does it differently), and if so then open it up and extract the installable theme zip file.

The easy way to tell is that if there is a zip file inside of the zip file named exactly the same as your purchased theme, then extract that file to upload as the zip file for your theme. If that zip file doesn't exist inside of the zip file you downloaded from your theme developer, then you can just upload the original zip file to Wordpress to install it.

Next, log into your Wordpress installation and go to Appearance > Themes > Add New (button at top) > Upload Theme, then browse to the installable zip file on your computer and upload/install it.

UPLOAD YOUR CHILD THEME AND POSSIBLY MAIN THEME FOLDERS VIA FTP

Once you have created your child theme, you need to upload it from your local computer to your web server. You do this by using the Internet standard File Transfer Protocol (FTP). There are many desktop programs that utilize FTP that allow you to upload and download files to and from your web server. Setting yourself up to be able to use FTP right now is in your best interest.

To setup an ftp account you need to create it in your cPanel. Once logged in to cPanel do a browser search (ctrl-f for find) for ftp. It is usually at Files > FTP Accounts. Go there and create your FTP login. In the section that asks for the path for this account make sure it is blank. This allows you to have access to all of the files and folders in your Wordpress installation. Once you've done this you'll need ftp client software that is installed on your local computer. I use FileZilla (https://filezilla-project.org/). Download and install FileZilla, then add a new site and your new FTP login to it then you can move files back and forth between your computer and your web server.

Next you need to extract the theme files from the zip file. Place them into a local folder like:

/WEBS/YOURDOMAIN/WP-CONTENT/THEMES/ORIGINAL-THEME-NAME/

Open FileZilla and enter your ftp login info. You'll also need the Host, which is usually ftp.yourdomain.com, and the port. The host can also be the IP address of your web server which is usually on the left-side information section of your cPanel. Just leave the FileZilla port set to its default value.

Once logged in you'll see left and right side panes. The left side shows your local drives and folders, and the right side is the web server files and folders. Browse to the location where you unzipped the theme files on the left side and on the right side browse to the folder /public_html/wp-content/themes/. Then drag and drop your local theme folders (and files inside them) into the themes folder on the right.

After you've uploaded the theme files, you need to activate the theme in Wordpress. Log into Wordpress then go to Appearance > Themes, select your new theme and activate it.

The significance of this effort is that every page of your site will use the theme folder defined above, which includes your main keyword, like Denver photographer. This is great for SEO. You want to be at the top of the search engine results page when people do a Google search for denver photographer, don't you?

An extra step that I always go through is to grab the setup and installation files that are usually in the original theme zip file and install them on the live site at http://yourdomain.com/setup. This gives you quick access to the theme setup and management instructions.

Follow these steps to upload your child theme:

1. Upload the three child theme files to your Wordpress themes folder. There will then be two themes in the themes folder:

/WP-CONTENT/THEMES/ORIGINAL-THEME-NAME/

/WP-CONTENT/THEMES/CHILD-THEME/

2. Activate your new Keyword Phrase child theme by logging into Wordpress and navigating to Appearance > Themes, selecting your child theme then activating it.

3. Problems or questions? You can find more information about creating child themes from the

Wordpress site in the Wordpress Codex[5]. The Wordpress Codex is the documentation site for the code used to construct Wordpress. The Wordpress code languages and technologies used are PHP, CSS and a MySQL database.

---

5 "Child Themes", https://codex.wordpress.org/Child_Themes

WRITING CONTENT THAT SOLVES YOUR CUSTOMER'S PROBLEMS

All of the effort you go through to get your website can be for naught if your content isn't appropriate. Your site visitors are looking for professionals who can help them solve their problems. Someone they can trust and ideally work with for years. That's what everybody wants. Everybody. Show them that you can help them accomplish their goals and solve their problems by the content on your site and you have them halfway in the door. The other audience for your content is search engines. They don't contact you, they give you better rankings if they like your content. Those rankings are important to your business because they can bring you customers.

Writing content that your visitors will appreciate and act on that also results in top organic search engine rankings is not difficult. I describe how to do it below. If you don't do it right then all of this time building a website will be wasted. Good content is that important.

WHAT CONTENT SHOULD YOU WRITE?

In the sections below I'm going to give you a lot of background and tactics about writing quality content. In this section I'm going to describe for you the content that your site visitors will consume voraciously and cause them to become raving fans.

Writing content is the biggest wall that my customers have run across through the years. It has stopped them from having a quality website and from gaining conversions, sales and new customers from it. The solution is, however quite simple.

Your customers come to you because they trust that you will provide the solution that they are looking for, or so desperately need. Where do you get the ideas for the content that they are looking for? *From the solutions you have already provided for your existing or past customers.*

Here's what I suggest:

1. Have everyone in your company list the solutions they have provided to customers.
2. Compile and prioritize the entire list by the most benefit provided to your customers.
3. Group the solutions as is necessary. They'll fall into natural groupings that can represent a series of articles/posts.

This is usually enough information to keep you busy writing for months. Not only that, it represents a body of work and services that your company excels at. As you're organizing the series of posts that you'll be writing keep in mind that you want to identify the customer pain points *and the words they'll use when they're looking for a solution*. I suggest typing the questions or search terms into Google and taking note of what Google suggests like this:

The terms they suggest are those that people are actually searching on. This gives you a lot more insight into what terms to use in your content.

Once you have your punch list of articles to be written, the logical next step is to determine what angle to take in writing them, what actually strikes a nerve with your audience to the tune of your readers massively sharing your article. One of my business partners, Pedram Shojai at http://well.org writes voluminously, and the articles he writes get a lot of attention and shares. In order to demonstrate what type of articles that people react to I directed him to BuzzSumo and do a search for anxiety. Here are the current results for that search:

Note that the top two articles have each been shared more than a million times on Facebook alone. If you curated (content curation explained below) those articles on your own blog then shared it in social media you can expect results better than if you have just dreamed up a new topic and wrote about it.

BuzzSumo requires a very reasonable paid subscription at $99/month to fully utilize the complete set of tools they provide, but they also provide a 14-day free trial on all of their subscriptions. I suggest that you get your list of solution-based articles from above together, sign up for the 14-day trial at BuzzSumo then research each of the articles all at once. Put all of the research into a Word doc along with screenshots and links to the top-rated articles so when it comes time for you to write the articles, you have the research completed, and all you have to do is write or curate the article without having to determine the details of the direction of the content. You should be able to do all of it within the 14 days, but if not then $99 for one month is a small amount to pay in order to ensure that your content has the biggest chance of striking a viral chord with your audience.

Another major boost you can get from BuzzSumo is to click the View Backlinks and View Sharers buttons to see who has engaged with the listed articles. *The same people may be interested in linking to and sharing your article!* This is only available in the paid version, but it is a great reason to get the 14-day trial and make serious use of it. Again, paying $99 for one month will allow you to get a lot of research done.

POWERFUL AND PROVEN SEARCH ENGINE OPTIMIZATION (SEO) STRATEGIES

Search engine optimization (SEO) is the process of getting your website ranked in the unpaid section of the search engine results page (SERP). This is called organic rankings, as opposed to paid Pay-Per-Click (PPC) advertising. The paid ads are well marked on the SERP, if your search was for a local service, then those local listings will be after the PPC ads, and the organic rankings will be below that. Here is a typical search engine results page for a search for Denver automotive repair:

I have done SEO for many customers since the beginning of the Internet, and in one case I multiplied my client's revenues from half a million a year to $4 million dollars a year, an eight-fold increase. This is what my customer told me. That may not even be possible with SEO today because of the competitiveness on the Internet, but I am mentioning it to show you that I am very familiar with the concept, and can point you in the right direction as far as integrating SEO concepts into your website content.

Clicks from sites that are ranked organically typically have great click-through rates and high conversion rates. This means that the #1, #2 and #3 positions in the SERP are very coveted by businesses. Here is a chart provided by Smart Insights[6] that illustrates that the top three organic positions get most of the clicks. This fact hasn't changed with time,

---

6   Chris Soames, "The Number One Spot – how to use the new search curve CTR data", http://www.smartinsights.com/search-engine-optimisation-seo/seo-analytics/the-number-one-spot-how-to-use-the-new-search-curve-ctr-data/

but the actual numbers vary based on the criteria described below.

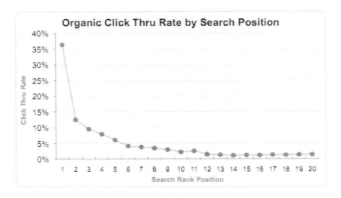

This chart shows that the top three positions garner 58.4% of the clicks. Actual clicks vary by:

- Country
- Date
- Branding vs. no branding
- Industry sector
- Age of the person doing the search
- Gender of the person doing the search

SEO has changed radically since its inception. At first all you had to do was list your site in places like Alta Vista or Infoseek and tweak your page content until it ranked #1. Infoseek showed the results of your changes in seconds. Then, when Google came onto the scene they said that links from other sites were a vote for your site, and they gave higher rankings to sites with a lot of links. Then they got picky. They said the links had to be relevant and from authority sites in your niche. They changed the ranking algorithm to penalize you if your site had spam links from sites like pharma or porn pointing to your site. Then they separated national or worldwide rankings from local rankings.

The Google ranking algorithm has many (thousands of) components and it is extremely complicated. I'm not going to go into any depth at all except to say that the methods and recommendations I'm providing below will always be a benefit to your company, regardless of Google rankings. Fortunately, they are also methods that result in top Google rankings today.

My perspective on this is that you should always do what is in the best interest of your company *as if Google rankings were not a factor in your efforts*. Write content that is in the best interest of your customers. The state of SEO today is that Google will recognize this and reward you with higher rankings. They want you to write for your customer and not just for Google rankings.

Incidentally, there are more search engines than Google, with Bing (by Microsoft) and Yahoo! rounding out the top three. A 2009 deal between Microsoft and Yahoo! means that Yahoo! results are now powered by Bing. How do Bing and Yahoo! play into SEO? Well, not much. Google gets the brunt of the search traffic on the Internet. Bing and Yahoo get some, but when you optimize your site and content for SEO you are mostly doing it for Google rankings. As of February 2016[7] Google's share of the search market is 64%, Bing and all Microsoft sites have 21.4%, Yahoo has 12.2%, the Ask network at 1.6% and AOL brings up the rear at 0.9%.

So, how do you get top organic rankings?

Organic rankings are the product of the strength of your onsite content and the quality of your offsite links and signals. You need both onsite and offsite efforts to get top organic rankings. If your website structure is strong and your onsite content is solid, optimized and structured well but you have no links pointing to your site then you won't get

---

7 "comScore Releases February 2016 U.S. Desktop Search Engine Rankings", https://www.comscore.com/Insights/Rankings/comScore-Releases-February-2016-US-Desktop-Search-Engine-Rankings, (March 16, 2016)

the top rankings. If you have a lot of authority links pointing to your site, but your content is thin, not optimized and not very interesting to a site visitor, then you won't get any top organic rankings.

That's not to say you won't appear in the Google at all, it just means that you won't get in *the top few positions*, which, as explained above is all that matters because they get the lion's share of the clicks and traffic.

If you know how and why to write good content then you can spend the same amount of time doing it right and getting results as you would by not learning this, so why not learn the basics then design and build your site with high-quality content to get rankings and enjoy the fruits of your labors?

There are many companies that follow Google's ranking factors and create tools and educational content such as Search Engine Watch, Backlinko, Search Metrics, Ahrefs, Moz, and many more. One of the differentiating factors for Ahrefs is that they have the largest third party (not a search engine) database of live backlinks available[8], and they pull information from the data in the form of reports that you can use to your advantage. This allows them to do detailed analysis of what works and what doesn't. Because of constant Google algorithm changes and rumors about their effect on a website's organic rankings, the analyses and reports provided by Ahrefs inject clarity into the fog of a complicated ranking algorithm and misinformation. Backlinko's specialty is of course, backlinks, or links pointing to your site from other sites, Backlinko disseminates information about how to get the best backlinks and articles illuminating the Google ranking algorithm.

---

8   https://ahrefs.com/

> *Two Data-Driven Approaches on How to*
> *Build Your Website and Create Content*
> *That Ranks At the Top of Google*

In this section I'm going to recommend actions for you based on key results from a couple of reports by Ahrefs and Backlinko. Ahrefs did two million keyword searches and analyzed the pages that were ranked at the top. Backlinko did one million searches to see what was causing the top rankings. It is a data-driven approach that you can act on directly to achieve the best rankings for your own website.

Here is a summary of the factors that will get your website ranked into the top positions in Google for your keyword searches based on the data-driven analysis.

Ahrefs

Ahrefs did an analysis of two million Google keyword searches to determine what on-page factors affect SEO rankings. Here's what they found:

1. Using your keyword in the URL has a negative correlation with rankings. Interesting. Basically, don't worry about placing your verbatim keyword into the URL of your page. When your search terms are in the URL of the top ranked pages then Google bolds those keywords in the URL when they show it in the search engine results pages (SERP), so that provides more opportunities to draw clicks. Focus on what the person reading the article will do. Use it to draw clicks or explain what's on the page, but don't stuff keywords into the URL for the purpose of SEO rankings. It is anti-productive.

2. Placing your exact-match keyword into the title also isn't as important as it once was. This is an *intent* conversation, in that, when someone does a search for a particular term then their reason for that search is now being interpreted by Google, and the pages

that Google determines are what they are really looking for are shown at the top of the SERP. Here is the example that Ahrefs provides[9]:

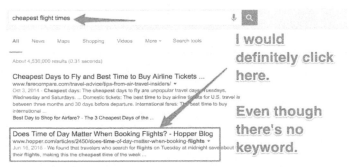

3. Meta-Descriptions – the Ahrefs study shows that placing your keywords in the description doesn't have an effect on your rankings, but I'm going to expand on that result here. When Google lists a page in their SERP, they usually take an excerpt from the pages for the text that appears below the blue link title that you click on to get to the page. Sometimes they take the meta-description that you provide for the page. This meta-description is an opportunity for you to draw a click from the person doing the search. Take that opportunity to craft a description that is intriguing enough for them to want to read more. Do this for all of your most important pages.

4. Use your exact match keyword in the h1 tag of your pages/posts. In Wordpress this means placing it into the page/post title at the top of the page as you're editing.

5. Break out your page/posts content into headings, sub-headings and sub-sub-headings using h1, h2, h3 tags for readability and don't worry about using your main keyword in the h2, h3, etc. tags. It is a

---

9   Tim Soulo, "On Page SEO in 2016: A (2M Keyword) Data Driven Analysis", https://ahrefs.com/blog/on-page-seo/, (June 21, 2016)

good idea to bullet out your content before you write any of it using these h tags, so you have a high-level roadmap that will accomplish your goals for the article.

6. Always use image alt and title tags, but not as a Google ranking concern. It is questionable as to whether the image alt tag is a page ranking factor, but the following two reasons for using alt and title tags are convincing:

   A. Not using image alt="" tags will produce an xhtml error. You don't want errors in your code.

   B. Image alt tags are required for section 508 accessibility compliance. Section 508 is a US federal government mandate that makes it easy for people with disabilities to read website content. In this case image alt tags are used by electronic readers that recite web page content for people without the blessing of sight.

   C. Using image title="" tags will open up a visual strip of text when site visitors run their mouse over the image. This is a usability benefit that your site visitors will appreciate.

7. Age of the page – older pages basically rank higher. I recommend that you look at your Google analytics and see what pages have brought the most traffic through time, then go back to those pages and update them to bring the content up-to-date to include appropriate calls to action pointing to your latest landing pages.

8. Shorter, descriptive URLs rank better than articles with long URLs.

9. Content length – the median length of #1 ranked content is about 750 words.

Backlinko

These observations are from a Backlinko analysis of one million Google search results[10] in regards to what factors are important for rankings:

1. Link to your page from different authority domains. The number of different domains linking to a page has the highest correlation to top rankings.

2. "Topically relevant" content that covers a topic completely and has at least 1,890 words tend to rank higher.

3. Having a secure certificate and using https for secure access to your website has been confirmed as a Google ranking signal.

4. Having at least one image correlates to rankings higher than pages with no images.

5. Pages with fast load times rank significantly higher than those that load slowly. Fast hosting and tweaking your own website with plugins, image optimizations and other page load time optimizations is worth the time and effort. Nobody wants to wait for a slow page to load, so page load time is a usability issue as well.

6. User engagement in the form of low bounce rates is still an important ranking factor. If your users engage with your content and spend time on your site then you'll be credited for it in the form of better Google rankings. Think engaging video.

---

10 Brian Dean, "We Analyzed 1 Million Google Search Results. Here's What We Learned About SEO", http://backlinko.com/search-engine-ranking, (September 2, 2016)

Subscribing to the email list of Brian Dean, the founder of Backlinko is one the best things you can do to be made aware of the strategies and tactics that are working today. Here is an example video that has three content hacks that *will* make a huge difference in the results you get from your website: https://www.youtube.com/watch?v=lyiikzjg9a0. Subscribe to his newsletter at http://backlinko.com. The information he disseminates to his email list is so important that the entire full screen of his home page is nothing but a signup form.

Mobile-Dedicated or Mobile Responsive Website?

On April 21, 2015 Google updated their algorithm to penalize websites that weren't mobile-friendly. Two months later it was determined that this was for mobile searches only, and not desktop searches[11].

What does mobile-friendly mean? It means that your site must be *fast,* and either mobile-dedicated, where the site is built specifically for mobile devices, or it must be mobile responsive where your site content re-arranges itself based on the width of the screen or the device viewing the page.

Having a mobile-friendly site is not just important for search engine ranking, it is important for your site visitors. Nobody wants to wait forever for a page to load, and consequently they don't. As noted above, a one-second delay can cause a 7% drop in conversions, so you should pay attention to this. Everyone has their phone in their pocket or purse, and they will be looking for your business on their smart phone. You want to be where they're looking and accommodate their visit with a website that meets their expectations in terms of performance and content layout.

You can test the mobile friendliness of your site at:

11 Jayson DeMers, "Post-Mobilegeddon Update: Is The Impact As Catastrophic As Predicted?", http://searchengineland.com/post-mobilegeddon-update-impact-catastrophic-predicted-221772, (June 18, 2015)

https://search.google.com/search-console/ mobile-friendly

The best way to make your Wordpress site mobile-friendly is to start with a mobile responsive theme. Coding responsiveness yourself is not a task for non-developers. As noted above in the *Picking a Wordpress Theme* section, there are many places to get premium and responsive Wordpress themes.

Solution and Success-Driven Keyword Research Strategies

Keyword research is one of the most important efforts that you must get right in order to ensure the success of your website. When you build your website you want it to be found by people looking for your products and services. Doing keyword research correctly is like going to the archery range, aiming at your target and firing off your arrow. Good chance of hitting your target. Doing keyword research wrong, or not at all, is like having someone tie a blindfold on you, spinning you around three times then telling you to shoot. The odds are not on your side, or your friends.

When you build a website you will always expect it to perform and doing appropriate keyword research is one of the important factors allowing you to accomplish this.

As a free download for buying this book I'm providing you a spreadsheet that lists forty-eight keyword tools I have used through the years, twenty eight of which are free. They have each served me at various times for different purposes. Each one is unique in terms of what they provide. For example, one tool provides a list of keywords that start with your typed in seed words then appends each letter of the alphabet to generate different keyword phrases like "your keyword phrase a...", "your keyword phrase b...", etc. Another tool provides a more creative list of possible long-tail keywords to provoke thoughts on your part like number lists (7 Simple ways...). One provides a pages keyword density for one, two and three keyword phrases. One show you keyword trends over time.

The keyword tool that I highly recommend and use the most is the Google Keyword Planner. You can learn straight from Google which keywords they deem relevant to your seed keywords and that you should be using in conjunction with them in your articles. You insert a handful of keywords that are relevant to your business, then Google will give you a list of typically 500 – 1,000 other keywords that *they recommend and are relevant to your seed keywords.* This makes it important to start with the right seed keywords. They produce keyword phrases that people are actually searching for. They also give you more golden information that allows you to know which ones you should focus on such as the following information:

- Average Monthly Searches
- Competition (low, medium of high)
- Suggested Bid

Note that the information provided by the Google Keyword Planner is based on *Google Adwords PPC campaigns historical information.* When you have a high number for each of these fields it means that your keyword is a hot commodity. They are searched for a lot, there are many bids for those keywords and people are bidding high for them. Ideally you'd be ranked very high organically for those keywords.

There is, however, information left out of the Google Keyword Planner data that is important to your business:

- **SEO competition** - as mentioned above, it is a lot more difficult to rank for broad and general terms than those that are more specific. SEO competition gives you numbers that you can use to determine whether a keyword has a reasonable amount of competition so you'll be able to achieve top rankings for it.

- **Dollar Value of the Keyword** – If the keyword doesn't have a high dollar value for organic rankings then it can possibly take a lot of work to get you ranked for it, with little return on your investment.

For those purposes I use Market Samurai, a desktop-based tool that gathers many competitive factors like SEO competition for the keyword in a pages title, content and URL. It draws its data from multiple sources like Google, Bing and Majestic SEO (an industry authority on the subject of online SEO tools) and is the tool I use for my final keyword analysis. Market Samurai's list of tools:

- Keyword finder and analysis
- Find competitor websites based on a keyword
- Domain finder based on the keywords you input
- Content finder and analyzer pulling from several sources
- Content publisher to your Wordpress and Wordpress.com sites
- *Find quality backlink opportunities* from several high-profile blogs, forums and Question/Answer sites

Their free trial also comes with a series of four videos that shows you how to use the tool most effectively to gain more website traffic with less effort.

If you do download the free trial of Market Samurai from the link above, then the next thing you need to do is export your keyword analysis data, convert the exported csv text file into your preferred spreadsheet format then add two new columns to the spreadsheet – Priority and Category. For every keyword I recommend that you add a 1 – 5 rating for the keyword where 1 is best in terms of your *business* priority. That gives you a business perspective on the value of the keywords. By placing a category for each keyword you'll have one more level of granularity when it comes time to use the keywords for an article you're writing and which category to use in Wordpress.

The Importance of Long-Tail Keywords, Intent and the Mobile Factor

When you use keyword phrases consisting of several words in them you have a much better chance of getting ranked for those keyword phrases. Not only that, you can incorporate the users intent in them. For example, let's say you were selling golf clubs. See the following keywords and note how the search terms get more specific and show more intent as you go down:

golf – Someone killing time on their computer

golf clubs – Someone doing general research for golf clubs

pitching wedge – Someone doing general research on pitching wedges

ping G30 driver deals – Someone looking to buy a Ping G30 driver

When doing your keyword research you need to think about what intent you are looking to capture, what specific types of products and services you *want to* provide. Of course it varies by the type of company. Here are some examples of long-tail keywords with intent to engage or purchase:

small business cpa firm to reduce our taxes

auto mechanic to fix my 2017 jeep grand cherokee transmission

chiropractor specializing in a stiff neck

whole roasted pig with green chile catering service (I must be getting hungry)

You need to keep the long-tail and intent concepts in mind when you do your keyword research and write your content. This refinement will make a huge difference in your results. In the above examples, if you instead had focused on cpa firm, auto mechanic, chiropractor or catering service then you'll not only *not be* targeting your company's specific services, but you'll be attempting to rank for keywords that are the most difficult to get top organic rankings for.

Now that we have really smart phones that you can just ask questions of like the Apple Siri or the Android "Ok Google…" capability, and devices like the Amazon Echo (Alexa) and Google Home, search engine queries are now being slanted to those coming from these devices. Now queries like these are becoming more important:

"Ok Google, what's the best Mexican restaurant near me?"

"Alexa, what are the best local activities for kids"

"What are the best local coffee shops"

People are searching on their mobile devices in a hands-free scenario looking for a service that they can use now. *They're on the way!* You need to think about these concepts when you compile your list of keywords that you'll be targeting for your website content.

The Best Tools to Find Long-Tail Keywords

Google again provides great methods and tools to acquire highly relevant long-tail keywords. Since it is Google rankings that you are after, taking Google's suggestions is getting your keywords straight from the horse's mouth.

Do a Google search for your topic and pay attention to the search terms that Google suggests in the search box:

Next, scroll down to the bottom of the results of your search and note the other terms (long-tail keywords) that Google suggests for you:

Searches related to concrete contractor

concrete **contractors denver**	**commercial** concrete **contractors denver**
concrete **delivery denver**	**good day** concrete
residential concrete **denver**	**denver** concrete **prices**
denver concrete **services**	**sunny day** concrete

Grab the keyword phrases that are relevant to your current needs and use them in your article. If you need more then recycle - take the relevant ones and use them in another search to get more suggestions.

A favorite tool among marketers is UberSuggest.io. You just type in a seed keyword, and it gives you a ton of other keywords by appending words to your seed keyword starting with each letter of the alphabet. The video at the bottom of the page shows you how to copy and paste these keywords to a spreadsheet and use all of their basic functions.

Another quick source of long-tail keywords is http://soovle.com. Just type in your keyword and they'll list relevant options from Google, Bing, Yahoo!, Wikipedia, Youtube, Answers.com and Amazon.

Many more keyword tools are available in the free download that you can grab from the Resources section at the end of this book.

Use Qualified, Prioritized Keywords to Drive Compelling Content

Once you have completed the above, then you have the information you need to start mapping out your website content. Create a Wordpress category for each of the categories in the spreadsheet. If a category is too broad, then break it down into multiple categories of finer detail. Sort the spreadsheet by two columns - priority then category. This provides you with the keywords most relevant to your business and the topics (categories) that you can provide solutions for. Next create a list of solutions representing a series of posts for each of the categories. You don't have to write the content now, just a list of concepts/solutions that you'll write about. This list will be your content map for future blog posts. Think in terms of problems that your customers are looking to solve, and solutions that you have already provided *or can provide*.

Ask each member of your team to make a list of the solutions they have provided for customers, then drop each one into the most relevant category. Doing this will provide a great inventory of blog posts that are targeted to solving your customers problems *with your company's priorities built-in*. They'll be customer-centric in terms of solutions to their problems, and they'll be focusing on keywords that are a priority to your business with a great chance of getting rankings and traffic from them.

This is huge, so if you didn't grasp this concept stop now. Go back and read it again. This is all of the content you'll ever need for your website. As you continue to provide solutions, add more content.

Important Places for Your Wordpress Content

Wordpress is a highly SEO-optimized website platform that can be even more optimized by making sure all of your posts are entered completely and correctly. I have built very SEO-optimized sites for customers only to see that they squander the SEO capabilities of Wordpress, and the overall success of their website by not taking the few extra minutes to fully optimize their posts. They simply don't enter all of the information necessary to get the maximum benefit of their posts and to get the page ranked in Google. It only takes a few more minutes to enter all of the information to get the attention of the search engines. I'll explain what you need to do to maximize the effect of your posts. You need to spend a few quality moments entering all of the details that will make the difference for your site. If you don't then all of the effort you put into building the site will go to waste, literally. A Ferrari with squirrel cage engine as it were.

Before starting to write your post you'll want to gather your list of the keywords that you want to focus on, with one in particular that you want to rank for, and several long-tail keywords to support it and that you also want to get rankings for. Keep in mind that trying to rank for top-level keywords such as insurance or mortgage is always going to be difficult. Use long-tail keywords as much as possible as explained above that include intent instead of littering your content with generic keywords. That will always be a fruitless effort.

To make sure that each of your posts is optimized to the hilt, make sure you have appropriate content in all of the following places for your posts:

1. **Post Title** – This is the text that appears at the top of the page between the <h1> and </h1> tags. It is the title that you enter at the top of the post in Wordpress. It obviously needs to be descriptive, and it would ideally contain your main keyword or a variation of it.

2. **SEO Title** – This is the title that appears in the search engines in a blue link. It's called SEO title because this is one of the main items on the page that is used for SEO rankings. Like the Post title, make it descriptive, and include your keyword.

3. **Meta-description** – this is the text that appears below the blue link in the search engine results page (SERP). The main focus of this section is to *draw a click* when someone reads it. Use your main keyword or variations in the meta-description.

A valuable tip for the SEO title and Meta-description: If you have run and optimized a PPC campaign at Google Adwords then use the ads that have drawn the most clicks as your SEO title and meta-description.

Here is an example SERP listing with the SEO title and meta-description. The description starts with a date. When you set your site up right (like I explain in this book) then you also get links to other relevant pages in your SERP listing:

Antique Furniture, Vintage Jewelry, Antique Art and Collectibles
coloradoantiquegallery.com/ ▾
Jul 29, 2016 - Denver areas largest **antique mall**, the Colorado Antique Gallery is a great place to find antique furniture, art, vintage jewelry and collectibles.
Visit Us · About Us · FAQ · Esther's attic antiques ...

4. **Main content** – Place your main keyword in the first paragraph, use long-tail keywords throughout the text and place the main keyword or a variation at the end of your main content. Make sure to cover your topic completely. Google penalizes sites that post thin content. A *cornerstone* article is one that is so complete in its coverage that it becomes a go-to source for the information in it and consequently many other websites link to it.

Break up the text into bullets and short paragraphs instead of long blocks of text. This is much better for Internet readers who are looking for succinct info bytes of content that they can skim instead of dissertations that take hours to read.

Posts with *relevant* images or videos get a lot more attention. As stated by Brian Dean of Backlinko in his video, Skyword noted that posts with images get 94% more social media views[12]. I highly encourage you to watch that video for excellent ideas on writing content. Make sure to sign up for Dean's email newsletter, and you'll be receiving valuable tips on writing great content that engages your visitors and gets top search engine rankings straight to your inbox. Brian Dean is one of the best.

 A. **Adding Images** – when you add images to the Wordpress media Library and your main content make sure to complete both the Alternative Text and Image Title Attribute for the image. Not entering alternative text for your image will produce HTML errors, and adding an Image Title Attribute will popup a little yellow strip of text with the title text when someone runs a mouse over the image. You can use the same text in each of these fields, and it would be ideal to use variations of your main keyword in them.

5. **Permalink** – Wordpress will create a permalink (or slug) which is the URL/address of the page/post when you first save it that looks like this: topic-of-your-article. You want to make sure your permalink is optimal, and if it isn't then click the edit link beside it and make it right. Make sure of the following:

 A. It isn't unreasonably long.

 B. It accurately describes the content of the post.

 C. It doesn't contain unnecessary stop words like the, and, of, or.

 D. It's not critical that you include your keyword per se, but at least some variation of it would be good for SEO.

---

12 Brian Dean, "This (Simple) White Hat SEO Strategy=59% More Traffic", https://www.youtube.com/watch?v=263xlymvLl4, (June 16, 2016)

6. **Categories** – think of categories as your website's table of contents. They are the main areas for your site content. Most of the sites I build use categories to place content on different pages like:

   A. Different book genres like true crime, mysteries, thrillers and romance.

   B. Different wellness categories like diet, exercise, mindset and medicine.

7. **Tags** – tags are one of the main SEO benefits of using Wordpress. When you place a tag on a post, Wordpress creates a separate page that lists all posts that use that tag. *That makes this page highly optimized for the words in that tag!* This is a topic that is many times dropped, and since it is simple to add tags there's really no excuse for it. Wordpress will suggest tags for you to use when you type in a seed keyword. You do not want to use tags for spamming purposes just like you don't want to stuff your posts with keywords to make them read like this "Our Thai food restaurant is the best Thai food restaurant in Destin and if you are looking for a Thai food restaurant then you can't go wrong with us." If you write your content like this then you'll get penalized and you'll be placed into a hole that may be very tough to dig out of. To determine if you should add a tag or not, if you feel that the trajectory of your website will mean that you'll be writing about a particular keyword phrase fairly often and there will be several other posts that will use it then ad a tag for it. If not then don't. Make sure to add a tag for the keywords you've targeted for each article.

8. **Sidebar** – in an ideal world every page and post on your site will have a sidebar that is specific to the topic of the content of that page/post. So many sites have generic ads or sidebar content that isn't relevant to the content of that page. That is a waste of space. When you plan your site content you

also need to plan the sidebars that you'll use on all of the pages and posts. If you have five major topics of your site then plan on five sidebars. Most Wordpress themes make it easy for you to create sidebars, and if the theme you select for your site doesn't have a simple way of managing sidebars then you can use sidebar plugins for this purpose. Relevance is everything. Make sure that you also place your offers *on every page of your site*. That means offering relevant products as well as asking for visitors to sign up for your email list so you can market to them directly.

9. **Featured Image** – although adding a featured image will not affect your search engine rankings, it is important in that the featured image will be used in blogroll pages like your blog page where an excerpt of your last ten images is listed along with the featured image. You should always set the featured image for your posts, and make sure it is relevant to the post. Generic stock photo images of people shaking hands are a turn off. Ideally use images that you have taken yourself that are on-topic and illustrate the point of the post.

DON'T FORGET THE STANDARD WEBSITE PAGES

When people visit a website they expect at least some kind of standardization. This doesn't mean you can't express individuality, great design and branding, but it does mean you should have certain content on your site that meets visitor expectations, so people can use your site effectively. This means you need to include certain pages for people to interact with your company.

The best way to determine exactly what content and information to put onto these pages is to research your competitors. Find your top competitors and open their FAQ,

Contact Us, etc. pages in multiple tabs in your browser. Make note of their content that is relevant and appropriate for your website, then create your own content *that is better than all of them.* As your site visitors peruse your company's services, website and offerings and compare them with your competitors you'll stand out from the pack.

Competitive analysis defines a target. It is very illuminating, and I guarantee that you'll find a lot of information that will improve your website and business. It is worth spending some quality time determining what your competitors are doing as far as their site layout and content. It can fill in gaps that you may not have thought of that will ensure that you don't forget a critical component that your site visitors and potential customers may be looking for.

These are the standard pages for every site in the typical order for the menus across the top:

- **Home** – since your home page gets the lion's share of traffic on your site you always need to make sure it represents your company in the most appropriate light.

- **About Us**

    o Privacy Policy

    o Terms of Service

- **Contact Us**

- **FAQ (Frequently Asked Questions)** - FAQ pages are very popular when people are doing their research, so you should think through questions you are always asked and provide thoughtful answers for each of them.

- **Reviews/Testimonials** - as many as you can get. Include people's full name, city, company name and company website address if appropriate. If you want your reviews to appear in a Google search along with five-star ratings then you can use a rich snippets plugin like the ones detailed in this post.

- **Blog** –blog pages have sidebars with information like previous posts, categories and tags.
- **Sitemap** – you can create a user sitemap with Dagon Designs Sitemap Generator.
- **Products/Services**
- **Case Studies**

Note that this is too many menu items to place in one line of menus across the top. I usually split them into two menu bars. I call them Corporate and Services. The corporate menus are grouped at the top, and the services menu items list your services across the main, bottom menu. By styling the lower menus you can make them bigger than the top menus so as to emphasize your products/services.

LANDING PAGES CAN EXPLODE YOUR CONVERSION RATES

Depending on your website goals, you may want to consider adding some landing pages to your site. Landing pages are special purpose pages optimized for the purpose of maximizing conversions. A conversion can be making a sale, be completion of a form, sending you an email or picking up the phone and calling you. Landing pages are the page that someone lands on when they click on a pay-per-click (PPC) ad – when it's done right.

By following the processes below, our team has reached conversion rates higher than 50% multiple times. Mind you, it doesn't happen overnight, but a methodical approach to your testing will always achieve great results.

Important landing pages items are

1. A compelling offer. This is many times the make or break item that can draw huge conversion rates,

or be the reason for tepid results. It is the single most important consideration for your landing page content.

2. All of the benefits of your offer
3. All of the features of your offer
4. Headline
5. Sub-headline
6. Product description
7. Your most powerful reviews and testimonials
8. Certification, association logos – this demonstrates your authority in the industry
9. Photos of the product/service
10. Photos of your team
11. Your phone number

In the initial stages of your landing page design processes you need to review your competitors' landing pages. What they offer, how they position themselves and what content they are emphasizing is important to know. Take this research and improve on it. Make your offer more compelling and paint your company in a brighter light.

The initial stages of landing page design consist of gathering all of the info above. You can place all of the landing page content into a common folder like Dropbox that can be shared by your team.

When you have gathered multiple offers, photos, testimonials, etc., which ones do you put onto your landing page? *All of them!* You want to know what combination of content results in the highest conversions. To do this you have to test the content.

Split-Testing and Multivariate Testing of Your Landing Page Content

After you have gathered all of your landing page content you need to test to see what content converts the best. One method is called split-testing or A/B testing. This pits one option against another. When one converts at a statistically significant higher number (like 90% better) then you stop the test, swap out the content that failed and replace it with another. Split-testing is the best method to use when you don't have a lot of traffic.

Once you have tested all of your offers, test your images. When you've tested all of your images, test your headlines, then subhead lines, benefits, features, etc. After you have tested all of the content you inventoried in your landing page analysis then you can go to the next step of rolling out to more channels to bring traffic to the optimized landing page with the higher conversions.

Through the years I have used many plugins to do my split-testing. You might want to try the Simple Page Tester plugin https://wordpress.org/plugins/simple-page-tester/. This article lists several other split-test plugins including Simple Page Tester https://premium.wpmudev.org/blog/ab-split-testing/.

When you have tons of traffic, either because you pay for it through PPC advertising, or you just get a lot of organic, free traffic to your site, then multivariate testing is a great method of optimizing your landing page content. Multivariate testing loads all of your variations into a testing system at once. Each item (offer, header, image…) are randomly served to page visitors. The analytics track what *combination* of page objects converts the best. It ends up that all of the content on the page work in concert with one another to ultimately cause the visitor to make a decision to convert or not. That is why I prefer multivariate testing. A great and reasonably priced multivariate testing tool is Visual Website Optimizer. It makes it easy to get started and track your results.

Third-Party Landing Page Tools

Another option to build and test landing pages is to use a tool built to do all of it. The main benefit of this is that you're using a tool from a company that does nothing but create landing pages and tools that convert at the highest level. I have written a blog post with a list of many landing page tools that you should check out: http://www.21stsoft.com/landing-page-tools-to-increase-conversions/.

I'll expound on one that I have used a lot – LeadPages. net. LeadPages offers you many templates to choose from, and the ones they offer *have been proven to convert at the highest rates after millions of page impressions and conversions.* It's impossible to do the same level of testing that their pages have been through. Another sweet feature is that it is easy to integrate their pages into your Wordpress website. Instead of sending clicks to a strange URL you can send them to one of the pages on your website. Their pages are simple to setup and get your content into them. This tool alone can change your company.

A Final Note on Landing Pages

In the Keyword Research section above, I detail a plan for creating your website content. There is one very important factor I didn't detail, and that is conversions – determining the keywords, ads and landing page content that convert the best for you.

What you can do *before you build your website* is use LeadPages.net or a similar tool to create a landing page then Google Adwords to bring traffic to it to see what keywords, ads and landing page content converts the best. Do this for every product and/or service you provide.

Once you have these results, create your website content around those results. Use the landing page directly, or use the content of them to create more website content. Add calls to action in appropriate places all over your site that funnel visitors to your proven landing pages. Use the ads that drew the most clicks in your calls to action and the title and meta-description of your pages and posts. That way, the page is listed in a search-engine results page, and the title and description of the listing is what has already been tested to draw clicks.

If you go this route then you'll build your website with content that has been proven to convert the best *for you!* If you test five of each of the landing page components like your offer, headline, sub-headline, photo, description, list of benefits and list of features, then the content that has tested to convert the best is the 1 in 78,125 combination that converts the best. If you build your website without first testing it with landing pages and PPC, then what are the odds of putting up content that will convert like this? One in 78,125.

Landing page optimization is a guaranteed method of creating content that meets your company's goals.

CONTENT CURATION ENHANCES YOUR AUTHORITY AND MAKES YOU MORE PRODUCTIVE

Content curation is the process of writing about and referencing content that others have written. Sometimes that content may even be on your competitors' websites. Yes, your competitors. Why would you do this you ask? Because it instills a sense of trust from your readership. When people see that you are posting content that is in *their* best interest, they are a lot more apt to read more of the content you post.

What you want to do is find the content that your ideal prospects/customers would like to read. Content that solves their most nagging problems. You'll give them credit with a link to their original post, and you'll write a blurb tying it into your own business and scenario. There are tools you can use to make this effort more efficient, like Scoop.it. It is a paid service, but well worth it if you spend hours creating quality content. This is a Scoop.it graphic that shows the anatomy of a well-designed, curated post. It is from their white paper "How to Blog Consistently in 30 Minutes a Day or Less".

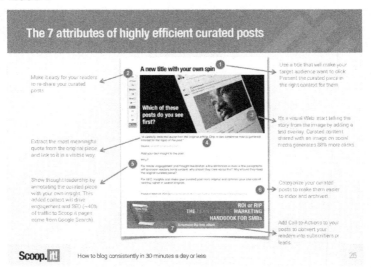

From the same paper, see the returns of content curation vs. content *creation*:

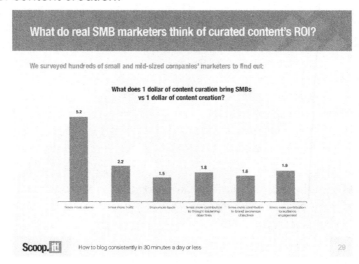

So, comparing content curation to writing all of the full articles yourself:

- You are able to publish 5 times more articles.
- You get twice the traffic.
- You get 50% more leads.
- Your thought leadership doubles.
- You get 60% more brand awareness.
- Audience engagement doubles.

You seriously need to integrate content curation into your website and content marketing plans.

TOP SEO EXPERTS TO FOLLOW AND CONTENT RESOURCES

If you're serious about writing content that will perform for you, then I recommend you get on these email lists:

http://neilpatel.com/   Neil Patel

http://backlinko.com/   Brian Dean

http://incomediary.com   Michael Dunlop

http://www.copyblogger.com/content-marketing/

"It's fast, it's free, and it delivers the finest online marketing education on the planet."

I have subscribed to hundreds of eNewsletters and taken many courses through the years. Each of these are guaranteed to educate you on how to write the best content out there. They each write detailed emails and blog posts based on their successes, so this would be cutting straight to the heart of the matter.

LOCAL SEO REQUIRES YOU JUMP THROUGH EXTRA HOOPS, BUT THE BENEFITS ARE MANY AND MAKE IT A NO-BRAINER

After many years of SEO meaning one thing, and that is the process of getting national rankings, SEO has splintered into two separate factions. One is for general nationwide rankings, still called organic SEO and rankings, and the other is now known as local SEO. If your customers are all within a few or several miles from your place of business, then you are defined as a local business. Typical local businesses are dentists, restaurants, bars, plumbers, electricians and pharmacies.

Local SEO includes all of the topics and ranking factors mentioned above for organic SEO, but it also includes several factors over and above those organic factors that are required for top local rankings. Indeed, top local rankings correlate very highly with top organic rankings. Of the factors that have the most affect on your local ranking, I'll list here the ones that you can most easily control to get the best local SEO rankings[13]:

1. **Top organic rankings** – do what I recommended above to accomplish this.

2. **Online reviews**, especially those in your Google My Business account.

3. **Links in the form of _consistent_ mentions of your business** name, address and phone number (NAP) placed into the top local citation sites and directories including Google My Business. Note that this does not mean backlinks. Organic SEO is

---

13   Dan Leibson, Vice President Local & Product, Local SEO Guide, "How Does Google's Local Search Algorithm Work?", http://www.localseoguide.com/guides/2016-local-seo-ranking-factors/, (June 23, 2016)

about the backlinks pointing to your site from other sites relevant to yours. Local SEO is about simply mentioning your company's information in online authority websites where people are looking for your services. These citation listings may or may not contain your website address, but a consistent listing of your company NAP is what's most important here.

4. **Having a mobile or mobile responsive website**. Mobile responsive means that your site content re-arranges itself based on the width of the screen viewing it or whether the device viewing it is a mobile device or not. For example, a typical responsive re-arrangement of your content goes like this. Keep in mind that it is up to the developer of your Wordpress theme as to exactly how your page content is re-arranged when a thinner screen or mobile device is detected:

   A. The menus squash into a tappable "hamburger menu" with three lines one on top of the other that are about the width of an underscore _. Here is what a hamburger menu looks like on a mobile device:

   B. The sidebar moves to be under the main content.

   C. If you have multiple footer boxes in a row then they are placed under the sidebar content, one footer box under the other.

I'll detail each of these items next, except for top organic rankings which has already been discussed above.

CODE YOUR COMPANY NAME, ADDRESS AND PHONE NUMBER (NAP) IN SEARCH ENGINE RECOGNIZED CODE

This is particularly important if you are a local company – one whose customers are within say five to fifty miles of your business location. This effort is in conjunction with the Citations section described below. Since local SEO is dependent on your company's name, address and phone number (NAP), having it on your website coded so search engines will recognize it and compare it with the citation directory listings is important. When the search engines see your NAP coded correctly on your website, they use it as the basis to look for your NAP in the important local citation directories. There are many, and they include sites like Yelp, Yellow Pages, CitySearch, Manta, Facebook, Yahoo Local and the Better Business Bureau. When they see your NAP coded correctly on your website, then they see you listed in those citation directories, it validates your company and the search engines give you credit towards your local rankings. When you couple that with positive reviews in all of the directories most relevant to your business in your city, and great content from/about your business in each of those listings, you will achieve a powerful local online presence that places you above your competitors.

The website at http://schema.org is the standard for the code you need to put onto your website. Here is some example code from schema.org that you can use in the footer of all of your websites pages, which is where I recommend that you place it. Of course, swap out my company information with yours:

```
<div style="" itemscope
itemtype="http://schema.org/
LocalBusiness">

<b><span itemprop="name">Your Business
Name</span></b><br />

<span itemprop="description">A company
```

```
description to spark intrigue and
cause people to click through to
your website to see your services</
span><div itemprop="address"
itemscope itemtype="http://
schema.org/PostalAddress"><span
itemprop="streetAddress">123 Main
St.</span><br />

<span
itemprop="addressLocality">Lakeside</
span>, <span
itemprop="addressRegion">CA</span>
<span itemprop="postalCode">98765</
span><br />

Phone: <span
itemprop="telephone">(789) 654-3987</
span><br />

<a itemprop="url" href="http://
yourdomain.com">Your Business
Name link text</a></div><img
itemprop="image" style="display:none;"
src="http://yourdomain.com/logo.png"
alt="Your Business Name, Category"
/><span style="display:none;">Price
Range: <span
itemprop="priceRange">$$</span><br
/></span><span itemprop="name">Hours
of Operation</span>

    <meta itemprop="openingHours"
content="Mo-Su 8:00-18:00">Daily 8am
- 6:00pm
</div>
```

Alternatively you can use the schema generator at:

http://schema-creator.org/organization.php

There are multiple types of code script that can be used, and the tool above uses JSON-LD.

THE AUTHORITY AND PERSUASIVE POWER OF ONLINE REVIEWS

The importance of the *process of purchasing products* has been recognized by corporations and manufacturers for many years. Since the Internet came onto the scene, this process has changed dramatically. I'm going to discuss how it has been recognized, formalized and changed, and what this means to you. Although it is not directly about building your Wordpress website, it is so important that it can literally be the make or break factor in your overall online success.

In 1986, a ground breaking book named *Moments of Truth* was written by the former President of Scandinavian Airlines, Jan Carlzon. In this book Carlzon posited that there are many moments that make up the ultimate purchase of a product, and some are more important than others. It is imperative that you win those moments from your competitors in order to survive and stay relevant. Carlzon believed in cutting management levels and empowering people in the front lines that work directly with customers to make decisions that otherwise would have been handled by mid-level or upper-level managers[14]. In 1978 at the age of 36, Carlzon took over the Swedish national airline Linjeflyg as president. In 1980 he became CEO and in 1981 he was President/CEO of the SAS Group, the holding company for the national airlines of Denmark, Norway and Sweden, better known as Scandinavian Airlines System (SAS). When he took over Linjeflyg they were hemorrhaging money to the tune of $17 million a year. Within a year SAS became Europe's most punctual airline, and in 1983 SAS profited $54 million[15].

---

14 Ed Burghard, "Three Moments of Truth", http://strengtheningbrandamerica.com/blog/2011/02/three-moments-of-truth/

15 Jan Carlzon, Wikipedia, https://en.wikipedia.org/wiki/Jan_Carlzon

After this dramatic turnaround SAS was named Airline of the Year for 1983 by Air Transport World[16].

Procter and Gamble CEO A.G. Lafley, called "one of the most lauded CEOs in history"[17] formalized and integrated the first and second moments of truth that Carlzon wrote about into the P&G sales and marketing processes to the tune of appointing a Director of First Moment of Truth, or Director of FMOT[18].

The three moments of truth are[19]:

1. First moment of truth: when a consumer sees a product on the store shelf and compares it to its competitors.

2. Second moment of truth: when the consumer takes the product home and uses it.

3. Third moment of truth: what the consumer does after experiencing the product. That can be complaining to the company or telling their friends or social media connections what a great/terrible product it is.

In 2011 Google introduced the concept of the Zero Moment of Truth, or ZMOT[20]. ZMOT is the research consumers pursue before they get to the store shelf. They search for your products and services online, and many times with their mobile device. Depending on the product, service

---

16 Airline of the Year - Winners, http://atwonline.com/airline-year-winners

17 Jennifer Reingold, "P&G Chairman A.G. Lafley Steps Down-For Good, This Time?", http://fortune.com/2016/06/01/pg-chairman-a-g-lafley-steps-down-for-good-this-time/, (June 1, 2016)

18 Emily Nelson and Sarah Ellison," In a Shift, Marketers Beef Up Ad Spending Inside Stores", Wall Street Journal, http://www.wsj.com/articles/SB112725891535046751

19 "Moment of Truth (marketing)", https://en.wikipedia.org/wiki/Moment_of_Truth_(marketing)

20 Jim Lecinski, "ZMOT: Why It Matters Now More Than Ever", https://www.thinkwithgoogle.com/articles/zmot-why-it-matters-now-more-than-ever.html, (August 2014)

or company they are researching they may only do a few searches, or they may perform dozens of qualifying searches before they make a purchase.

All of this adds up to three important factors *that you must consider* for success in today's online world:

1. As Woody Allen said, "Showing up is 80% of life"[21]. If you aren't where your customers are looking for your products then you simply lose outright. *They will do their ZMOT research*, and you desperately need to be where they are looking, or you're dead. You basically don't exist to them.

2. If you are there but have a poor showing then you lose again. Who will purchase from a company that appears everywhere they look and has nothing but loud complaints from previous customers? Not me.

3. If you are everywhere they are looking *and you show a strong presence with many reviews and a very high average five-star rating* then you have already accomplished a lot of the job of your sales team. You'll get the call because you have impressed them, as you have impressed your other customers who appreciated your service so much that they wrote a glowing review of your company. They aren't consciously thinking through all of the details that I'm presenting here, but you convinced them because of your outstanding online presence and convincing honest reviews. You have already prepared them to buy from you, so when they do call they'll just be asking final qualifying questions since they have seen that your previous customers are delighted with your product and service.

So, how do you win the ZMOT game? Be where your potential customers are searching and present a compelling and positive presence in terms of many honest four and

21 Showing Up Is 80 Percent of Life, http://quoteinvestigator. com/2013/06/10/showing-up/, (June 10, 2013)

five-star ratings from real customers of yours. It isn't rocket science.

How do you accomplish this? Search for your services and take note of what sites list service providers. Create accounts in all of those sites, and provide your customers with links to those sites so they can provide honest reviews. Sites that you'll see include Google My Business, Yelp, Yellow Pages (yp.com), City Search, Manta, Houzz, Home Advisor, Super Pages, Dex Knows, FourSquare, Facebook and the Better Business Bureau. There are many others, and ones most important to your business change based on your business vertical, your city and country. For example antiques.com is more important to an antique company than a local florist.

The Benefits of Negative Reviews (Believe it or Not)

Before I move on to the next important topic of discussion of citations, I want to mention the value of negative reviews. Some companies obsess with their five-star reviews. It ends up that negative reviews can actually legitimize the rest of the reviews your company has on a citation site. If all people saw was a string of glowing five-star reviews then they'll think something is up – and many times they'd be right. I have seen other companies wrangle over a bad review when their previous reviews have all been five-star ratings. I have seen companies enraged over a bad review that disparages them so badly that they contact Google to get the review disqualified and removed. If the review is against Google's terms of service then sure, dispute it. If not then you should just suck it up and focus on getting more positive reviews by asking happy customers to provide reviews for you and making it easier for them to do it. If the bad review happened because of a real problem at your place of business, then I suggest you fix the problem.

I had a company contact me about reputation (review) management because of their terrible average five-star online ratings. Their ratings were averaging two to 3.5

stars and they wanted me to fix it. They were hoping for a quick fix that could bring them to a 4.5 average star rating everywhere. When I checked out their entire online presence, it was obvious that the problem was based on bad service. They had been in business for twenty years, and people had been placing reviews online for their company as soon as it became possible for them to do so. I explained how I could grease the tracks and make it easier for his customers to provide reviews, but the positive or negative nature of the reviews is up to the customer, and ultimately dependent on the quality of service. Regardless I explained, a change would not happen quickly because with so many negative reviews, it would take a long time to overcome them and increase the average rating. He didn't engage with me because he was bent on obtaining quick results. I explained to him the risk of pursuing this direction (more on this topic below), and we went our separate ways.

When people are researching your products and services, they'll many times go to the negative reviews first. If not first then they'll make it there eventually. They want to see if the problems that have arisen are relevant to them. One example is when one of our true crime authors at WildBlue Press got a one-star review that said the author was always citing sources for the statements he had made, and the reviewer was annoyed by them. It ends up that many people who read true crime books want to know that they are actually true, and those citations provide real evidence that the author did his job.

It's the same for any other product or service that people search for online. They'll go to the negative reviews to see if their particular situation is relevant to the negative reviews. It may be specific to a job, it may be cost, timeliness, friendliness or quality of the final paint job. People will check out the negative reviews to make sure that they aren't relevant to their own needs and situation. *Sometimes they'll even disregard a relevant negative review if there are so many positive reviews that are meaningful to their current needs.*

There is another concept that most people realize and understand, and many times they have discussed with others. Even if they have not realized or mentioned it before, the concept of "some people can never be satisfied" is very real. When people read negative reviews, some of them will be from a person that obviously just had a bad day and needed to rant. These type of reviews are recognized by people searching for your services, and their presence actually legitimize the rest of the reviews you have.

Don't be concerned about less than five-star or negative reviews *as long as they are not about real problems with your business or customer service!* If they are truly about problems with your business, then you need to fix those problems immediately. This is why actually managing your online reviews is critical to your long-term growth. This means you are notified each time a review of your company is placed online. It doesn't cost much to manage online reviews on a monthly basis, and you should consider it if you are in it for the long-term. You can always contact me to discuss the many options available including no cost and other options that cost less than $100 a month.

A couple real benefits of *managing* negative reviews (and knowing when they happen) are

I. They allow you to see problems and act on them, meaning talk to an employee about that specific problem to make sure it doesn't happen again, and *maybe* respond to the bad review online. I say maybe because you have to be extremely cautious of doing this. *Absolutely NEVER* strike up an argumentative correspondence with anyone that has left a negative review online. That will only cause more problems for you, *and it's in front of the world.* If you are going to respond to a bad review simply explain to them that you have addressed and corrected the problem and you appreciate their business. You might even offer them a discount as a good faith gesture on the same service when they return. There is a lot of qualified commentary online about responding to negative reviews, and if you are in this situation then I recommend researching it further before actually doing it. It can save you a lot of grief, and the loss of years of hard-earned customer goodwill.

2. They prove that you aren't "stuffing the ballot box" (see next section) with a lot of fake reviews. When people see a dozen five-star ratings and no others they they're always wary of someone contacting all of their friends (only eight?) and having them submit 5-star ratings.

Warning – Don't Stuff the Ballot Box!

A few words of warning: many people think they can "stuff the ballot box" by asking their friends and family for 5-star reviews. Maybe they'll pay for five-star reviews outright, or reward people with gift certificates or other compensation for them, monetary or not, for providing glowing reviews. DON'T EVEN THINK OF DOING ANYTHING LIKE THIS! The search engines and local citation sites like Yelp and Google My Business are very skilled at detecting practices that are against this practice, which is against all of their terms of service. When they do bust a company that is trying to cheat the system like this they come down hard on them. The most compelling advice I have run across to fix the problem of Google penalizing a company for this type of offense *is to change your company name!* It's that difficult to get back into Google's good graces. You don't want to put yourself into that situation, so play fair and honestly. Doing so takes time to gather momentum, but it pays off in the end.

Provide a great service for your customers and make it easy to provide online reviews. That's just good business. It is not specific to Google or online rankings.

Reviews get you conversions and sales. The next section discusses citations which also bring conversions as well as local search engine rankings.

PUBLICIZE YOUR COMPANY NAME, ADDRESS AND PHONE NUMBER (NAP) IN CRITICAL CITATION DIRECTORIES

Local citation directories are where Google and the other search engines look for your company name, address and phone number (NAP) to validate that you are a real company that they should pay attention to. If you aren't on those sites where they look for local businesses, then you won't get the credit they have deemed to be important for legitimate businesses.

The following US Local Search Ecosystem diagram chart by MOZ[22] shows the interconnections between the main local citation sites. The ones listed with larger text for their name provide the ones with smaller text with the NAP data for local businesses. Logic would say that all you need to do is submit to the main providers like infogroup, factual or acxiom. It ends up that it's not that easy.

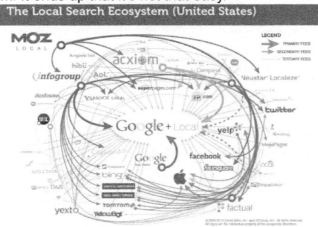

---

22   The U.S. Local Search Ecosystem, https://moz.com/learn/local/local-search-data-us, (2014)

What citation sites should you focus on? Those that are relevant to

1. **Your type of business** - for example Home Advisor is important to a contractor whereas Antiques.com is important to an antique business. Here is a list of the most important citation sites by the category of your business: https://moz.com/learn/local/citations-by-category.

2. **Your city** - different sites are important on a city by city basis. Here is a list of the most important citation sites by city: https://moz.com/learn/local/citations-by-city.

3. **Your country** – each country has a different set of important citation sites. This is a list of the top citation sites by country:

   http://searchengineland.com/top-50-citation-sources-for-uk-us-local-businesses-104938

There are many services that will list your company in the most important citation directories for your business. Here is a list of services I have used myself, and my take on them. They are all reasonably priced:

- SweetIQ.com – a natural, gradual placement of your NAP citation listings is what Google loves, and SweetIQ lists your site this way. They also monitor reviews of your company that appear in the citation sites, and provide you easy access to respond to them if you so desire. The listings stay when you terminate the service, which is very important. An excellent service from my experience.

- WLMarketing.com – a company that will list your NAP on a one-time basis in the number of directories that you pay for. They have varying levels of service and granularity in terms of the amount of information about your company that is listed. If you aren't going to be changing the information in your NAP citation directory listings then this is a good choice. They provide the list of citation directories that they'll submit to, but if your chosen directories are not in that list they'll work with you to submit to those also. Another excellent service.

- Yext.com – Yext submits your NAP listings to a comprehensive list of the most important citation sites, and it happens immediately. When you update your listing it is changed in all of them in real-time. They manage duplicates which can cause problems for your online rankings if duplicates aren't managed like this. The drawback of Yext is that if and when you terminate the service you lose all of those listings. The Yext advantage is that their service allows you to make real-time changes to your company listing allowing you to place seasonal offers that would be important to your business.

A detailed discussion of citation listing services and companies is provided in a great BrightLocal article written by Myles Anderson[23]. He breaks out the companies by direct-to-site submissions aggregator submissions and provides detailed tables of features and costs. I suggest you check out his article if you are going to pursue citations for your business (which, of course, I recommend that you do), and consider the companies listed above as well. They have worked out very well for my companies and those of my clients. Note that Yext is listed above and in the BrightLocal article as well.

I mentioned above that your name, address and phone number (NAP) are important bits of information that you want out there in the citation directories. NAP is an acronym coined in the industry because it is so important. I want you to realize that it is also important that you list your website

---

23 Myles Anderson, "Local Citation Services Compared – Moz Local vs. BrightLocal vs. Yext vs. Whitespark vs. Advice Local vs. Synup, BrightLocal", BrightLocal, https://www.brightlocal.com/2016/11/02/moz-local-vs-yext-vs-brightlocal-vs-whitespark/, (November 2, 2016)

address (URL - Uniform Resource Locator [of all things]) like http://yourdomain.com in all of the same places. Even though the search engines validate you with your name, address and phone number, the addition of your website address will give you valuable backlinks from the most important directories that will boost your local rankings. Make sure to include your website's URL in all of your listings!

Consistent and Accurate Citation Listings Are Imperative

Where traditional organic SEO focuses on *links* pointing to the pages of your site, Local SEO focuses on mentions of your business name and associated address and phone number in the most important citation directories and sites on the Internet. Those citations must be *verbatim* listings of your NAP information and website address. Different spellings of any of these items is interpreted by Google as a different company. *This will critically damage your local online rankings.* Using one of the services mentioned above is important to having consistent and comprehensive listings and coverage in the citation directories that matter the most.

Here are some examples of discrepancies that can cause problems that would cause search engines to recognize your company as a different one in the citation directories:

Company Name

Company Name, Inc

123 Main

123 Main St.

123 Main Street

http://yourdomain.com

http://yourdomain.com/index.php

http://www.yourdomain.com

https://yourdomain.com

Google My Business Listing Is the #1 Account To Claim

Because of its importance I'm mentioning that having a Google My Business account listing with all fields complete to include several appropriate images and the proper category is one of the most important factors in local rankings. If you haven't claimed yours yet, then do so here:

https://www.google.com/business/

HOW TO SPEED UP PAGE LOAD TIMES BY MULTIPLES

Ok, you've built a website and put great content into it. Is there anything else? Yes, site performance, meaning specifically page load times.

The benefits of making your pages load fast are

1. People love it when pages load quickly.

2. Search engines love it when pages load quickly.

3. People show their appreciation by staying to read your content and convert into leads or actually purchase your products and services.

4. Search engines show their appreciation by giving you better organic rankings.

These benefits make it worth the effort to speed up your page load times. This section guides you through the simple, no-brainer efforts as well as the technical changes that will make your website pages load quickly.

I was reviewing some new sales funnel content for usability and performance that our team at Well.org had created. One of the pages took 42 seconds to load. When I ran it at WebPageTest.org the culprit jumped out at me. It was an image that should have been a png or gif image no larger than 500 bytes. Instead, the image was 17 mb in size. After fixing it, the page took five seconds to load the first time, and 2.5 seconds on the second load after the content was cached.

That's the kind of results you can get when you take the time and use the right tools to analyze your site's performance. It's impossible to optimize maximally without the right tools, so I'll describe a few of them.

THE RETURN ON INVESTMENT (ROI) OF FAST PAGE LOAD TIMES

There is a tangible benefit and real monetary value to having a fast website. Nobody wants to wait for a slow page to load. Nobody. The ramifications of having fast page load times have been studied by some of the best companies out there. KissMetrics is one of them.

Here are several salient points from a KissMetrics infographic[24]:

- A one second delay in page load time (or three seconds of waiting) decreases customer satisfaction by about 16%.
- 44% of online shoppers will tell their friends about a bad experience online.
- 52% of online shoppers state that quick page loading is important to their site loyalty.
- 40% abandon a website that takes more than three seconds to load.
- 79% of shoppers who are dissatisfied with website performance are less likely to buy from the same site again.
- A one second delay in page response can result in a 7% reduction in conversions.

So, page load time is important, and it goes directly to your bottom line.

Some example dollar figures to consider:

If your site is making you $100,000 per month then you're losing $84,000/year if your site experiences a one second delay. In the case of a typical Wordpress twelve second page load time, when you reduce that to three seconds then based on the info from KissMetrics above, you can expect

---

24 Sean Work, "How Loading Time Affects Your Bottom Line", https://blog.kissmetrics.com/loading-time/

a $756,000/year increase in sales. Not to mention the improvement in visitor experience. Test your page load time at http://www.webpagetest.org/ to test your page load time performance and see what the possibilities for improvement are.

LET'S TURBO-CHARGE YOUR WEBSITE

First Back Everything Up!

There is a distinct possibility that problems will crop up in this page load time optimization process, so creating site backups is the logical first step.

There are a couple options:

1. Back up your database and all files in the themes, plugins and uploads folders. This will allow you to re-create the site in case of catastrophic failure. It happens. It has happened to me (I had backups). I have talked to many people that made major changes to the site and didn't back up first. Believe me, you'll be glad you have them. Details on backup options are in the Setup Wordpress Backups section below.

2. Even better, clone your website and make all changes to the cloned site. This gives you complete latitude to try anything you want with no risk at all. Once the website's performance is what you are aiming for you can deploy it to the live site. This is a completely safe way to tweak your sites performance. There are many Wordpress website cloning tools. I won't cover them here, but it is always good practice to have a development site ready for you to test and optimize without the risk of doing it on a live site. If you use this method then remember

to not change any content on the live site or you'll lose it when you make the optimized site live.

Baseline Your Site's Page Load Time Performance

The next step in optimizing your website's performance is to get a baseline of your sites current performance. You'll see the issues causing your page load time delays, and many times exactly how to fix them.

Use the tools in the next section to get a baseline of your website's performance before you start optimizing it.

Online Website Performance Testing Tools

Web Page Test: http://webpagetest.org

This is a great tool for an initial glance at the objects loading on a page in a waterfall diagram. You'll quickly see the objects that are taking very long to load and allow you to go straight to those pain points and correct them. A typical culprit is huge images.

Varvy Page Speed: https://varvy.com/pagespeed/

This tool provides a quick health check of your web server from several performance perspectives, many of which are addressed in the sections below. It gives you a Pagespeed score and a bird's eye view of whether you need to optimize your site or not. If most of the sections aren't checked then you know you have work to do:

GTMetrix: http://gtmetrix.com

GTMetrix gives you guidance on how to fix the issues with your site. It includes their PageSpeed score as well as a YSlow score and has a waterfall diagram. YSlow was created by Steve Souders who previously served as Google's Head Performance Engineer, Chief Performance Yahoo!, and Chief Performance Officer at Fastly. He wrote the groundbreaking book *High Performance Websites: Essential Knowledge for Frontend Engineers* that caught my eye one day and got me interested and involved in the subject of website performance several years back.

When you have an account, GTMetrix has the capability to create a video of your web page rendering that can also assist in determining bottlenecks.

On to the actual optimization effort.

IMAGE OPTIMIZATION PLUGINS

Images are typically the biggest culprit responsible for slowing down your web pages. It is so easy to upload images that are huge, and when you have many of them on one page it can kill your pages load time performance.

There are many plugins that can help you with this. I have tried several. Then last year I ran across this blog post at Elegant Themes:

https://www.elegantthemes.com/blog/resources/
best-wordpress-image-optimization-plugins

I have been using WP Smush for years which has worked great, but the plugin **Compress JPEG & PNG images** performed better in their tests, so lately I have been using it instead and it works great. You have to register with them then grab their API, but it costs nothing unless you want to optimize more than 100 images a month. I recommend that you use this plugin to optimize your sites images.

.HTACCESS OPTIMIZATION SETTINGS

The Wordpress .htaccess file is a text file that resides in the root folder of your website. Wordpress uses it as a virtual traffic cop to control virtual folder redirections when you create pages or posts with URLs like this: http://yourdomain.com/this-is-a-virtual-redirect-folder/.

.htaccess files have a lot more capabilities than that. For the purposes of this discussion, they are used to optimize site page load times and control the server so your site pages load as fast as possible, and the communication between the server and a browser is optimized to the fullest extent.

The settings suggested below will speed up your page load times the first time the page is loaded, and every time thereafter. You should simply add all of the code below to your .htaccess file.

At the end of this section is a snippet of code that includes all of the sections discussed below. You can just copy and paste it into the bottom of your .htaccess file. Note that, if your website resides on an nginx web server then .htaccess files are not supported.

IMPORTANT!

To access your .htaccess file, download it via ftp from your web server. Next, make a good copy of it and save it off to the side. Edit a separate file to be uploaded. This ensures that you have a backup in case of any mistakes or errors in the file you upload. *You can take your site down by making mistakes in this file.*

In case you cannot recover from .htaccess mistakes you can re-create a new one by logging into Wordpress and going to Settings > Permalinks > Common Settings then changing the permalinks setting to Plain and saving. After it has been saved, set it back to Post name and save again. That will re-create your .htaccess file.

Browser Object Caching

You can control how a browser caches the content like text, images and scripts that it receives from the web server. Caching the content means that, instead of having to load every page object required of a page to fully render its content, if the content had been previously loaded and cached, then the browser can pull these objects from the cache instead of requiring it to be sent from the web server again.

Use this code in your .htaccess file to enable caching on your server:

```
# Enable object caching
AddType image/x-icon .ico
<IfModule mod_headers.c>
# YEAR
<FilesMatch
".(ico|gif|jpg|jpeg|png|flv|pdf)$">
 Header set Cache-Control
"max-age=29030400"
</FilesMatch>
# WEEK
<FilesMatch ".(js|css|swf)$">
 Header set Cache-Control
"max-age=604800"
</FilesMatch>
# 24 HOURS
<FilesMatch ".(html|htm|txt|php)$">
 Header set Cache-Control
"max-age=86400"
</FilesMatch>
</IfModule>
```

Expires Header

When you cache content using the code above there needs to be a control telling the browser how long to look for the cached content. The expires header does just that. It doesn't come into play on the first page load because the objects haven't been cached yet. On the second and all subsequent page loads, however, the object hasn't timed out, and it is in the cache then the browser doesn't have to request it from the server. It grabs it from its local cache thus saving significant time to load the objects. Typical time savings are 50% – 70%. I'm testing a few of the websites I manage as I write this and that is a very realistic savings that you can expect when you properly set up your cache management.

This code adds the expires header capability to your .htaccess file:

```
# add Expires header
# from https://gtmetrix.com/add-expires-headers.html
<IfModule mod_expires.c>
# Enable expirations
ExpiresActive On
# Default directive
ExpiresDefault "access plus 1 month"
# My favicon
ExpiresByType image/x-icon "access plus 1 year"
# Images
ExpiresByType image/gif "access plus 1 month"
ExpiresByType image/png "access plus 1 month"
ExpiresByType image/jpg "access plus 1
```

```
month"

ExpiresByType image/jpeg "access plus
1 month"

# CSS

ExpiresByType text/css "access plus 1
month"

# Javascript

ExpiresByType application/javascript
"access plus 1 year"

</IfModule>
```

GZip

GZip is a method of compressing your website content before it is passed from your web server to the browser. When enabled, gzip capabilities are passed from the browser to the web server notifying the server that the browser can accept gzipped files. The server finds the requested files, gzips them up and sends them to the browser notifying it that the files are gzipped which causes the browser to unzip them and load then into the page for rendering.

Add this code to your .htaccess file to enable GZip compression:

```
# Enable GZip compression

  <ifmodule mod_deflate.c>

AddOutputFilterByType DEFLATE image/
gif image/png image/jpeg image/x-icon
application/pdf application/javascript
application/x-javascript text/plain
text/html text/css text/x-component
text/xml application/json </ifmodule>
```

Keep-Alive

Setting up your browser to server communications to enable keep-alive means that there isn't a unique back and forth communication (TCP connection) required for every object passed between the server and the browser. Also known as a persistent connection, keep-alive minimizes the back and forth communication required to load a web page and, therefore, speeds up your page load times.

Use this code in your .htaccess file to enable Keep-alive:

```
# Enable Keep-alive
# from https://varvy.com/pagespeed/
keep-alive.html
<ifModule mod_headers.c>
    Header set Connection keep-alive
</ifModule>
```

Entire Code Snippet To Copy and Paste Into Your .htaccess File

Save a copy of the .htaccess file contents, then copy the following code into the bottom of your .htaccess file and make sure to change the dates (for your reference). If the site breaks then put the original code back and troubleshoot. This code, along with all of the code mentioned in this book is available as a free download on the link to the resources page provided at the bottom of this book.

```
###### Added 7/7/20XX to speed up page
load times
# from https://www.bluehost.com/blog/
account-tips/the-ultimate-guide-
to-supercharging-your-wordpress-
blog-2097/
# Enable object caching
```

```
AddType image/x-icon .ico
<IfModule mod_headers.c>
# YEAR
<FilesMatch
".(ico|gif|jpg|jpeg|png|flv|pdf)$">
 Header set Cache-Control
"max-age=29030400"
</FilesMatch>
# WEEK
<FilesMatch ".(js|css|swf)$">
 Header set Cache-Control
"max-age=604800"
</FilesMatch>
# 24 HOURS
<FilesMatch ".(html|htm|txt|php)$">
 Header set Cache-Control
"max-age=86400"
</FilesMatch>
</IfModule>

# add Expires headers
# from https://gtmetrix.com/add-
expires-headers.html
<IfModule mod_expires.c>
# Enable expirations
ExpiresActive On
# Default directive
ExpiresDefault "access plus 1 month"
# My favicon
```

```
ExpiresByType image/x-icon "access
plus 1 year"
# Images
ExpiresByType image/gif "access plus 1
month"
ExpiresByType image/png "access plus 1
month"
ExpiresByType image/jpg "access plus 1
month"
ExpiresByType image/jpeg "access plus
1 month"
# CSS
ExpiresByType text/css "access plus 1
month"
# Javascript
ExpiresByType application/javascript
"access plus 1 year"
</IfModule>


# Enable GZip compression
<ifmodule mod_deflate.c>
AddOutputFilterByType DEFLATE image/
gif image/png image/jpeg image/x-icon
application/pdf application/javascript
application/x-javascript text/plain
text/html text/css text/x-component
text/xml application/json </ifmodule>
# Enable Keep-alive
# from https://varvy.com/pagespeed/
keep-alive.html
<ifModule mod_headers.c>
```

```
    Header set Connection keep-alive
</ifModule>
###### End of 7/7/20XX addition to
speed up page load times
```

MAINTAIN A HEALTHY DATABASE

As you add and delete content on your website, comments are added and deleted and content generally grows and is modified, the Wordpress MySQL database becomes inefficient. Gaps form in the file structure, indexes lose sync with the data in the database, and with time they cause database performance to slow down, and the capability to retrieve the right data diminishes. A database index is an internal structure that lists data in a table in a specific order. An example would be the White Pages book that the telephone company used to distribute to all households. The listings were in order of last name, first name. The data isn't entered into the database in that order, so a last name, first name index is used to print the listings in the right order.

There are multiple ways to close the gaps and inefficiencies in your database. It can be accomplished manually using your cPanel phpMyAdmin database management tool, or it can be done with a plugin like WP-DBManager.

Optimize the Wordpress Database Manually Using phpMyAdmin

If you're not a tech-type person then you might want to shy away from this one. I am describing it so you'll see one of the purposes of phpMyAdmin, which isn't a bad skill to have when you work with Wordpress.

If you do want to brave changing the database directly, then go to phpMyAdmin in cPanel then select your account username then Wordpress database on the left-side. You'll next see all of the Wordpress tables listed in rows. The far-right column is Overhead. For each row with a number in the Overhead column check the checkbox on the left-side of the row. When you've done this for all tables with overhead, scroll to the bottom and in the drop-down that says "With selected:" select Optimize Table, and after a few seconds your table will be optimized.

How To Retrieve Your User Password Directly From the Database Using phpMyAdmin

If you are completely locked out of your Wordpress site and can't login for whatever reason you, can go straight to the database and change it manually. This typically happens when a security plugin has gone wonky or your site has been compromised. If it happens to you then you should take other security measures, but for now I'll show you how to change your password.

Here's how:

1. Open phpMyAdmin in the Databases section of cPanel.

2. Click on the wp_users table.

3. Click the Edit link next to the user you want to change the password for.

4. Enter or paste your new password into the box to the far-right of the user_pass field.

5. In the Function column for the same row select MD5.

6. Click the Go button.

7. You now have a new password for that user.

Plugin to Optimize and Backup the Wordpress Database Automatically

The WP-DBManager Plugin is great for many reasons:

- It creates database backups that reside on your

server. You can set the number of backups stored on your server.

- It emails the database backup to you (if you so desire).
- It repairs the database and fixes errors or other anomalies that can occur in the database.
- It optimizes the database.

Although there are other plugins that have similar features, like WP-DB-Backup, WP-Optimize and DB-Optimize, the combination of features listed above is worth going with WP DB Manager. Those features are critical to the long-term viability of the database and, of course, your website.

After installing and activating the plugin go to Database > DB Options > Automatic Scheduling, then make these setting changes:

Automatic Backing Up Of DB:	1 Days	Gzip: Yes
Automatic Optimizing Of DB:	2 Days	
Automatic Repairing Of DB:	3 Days	

LIMIT THE NUMBER OF POSTS ON BLOGROLL PAGES

On your blog or category pages Wordpress lists your latest posts. This is called a blogroll. I have seen many sites where they list the entire post on the blogroll pages instead of an excerpt, and they list tons of posts, like 30 or 50. This slows the page load time down immensely. You need to limit the number of posts shown on the page, and to limit the content of each to be an excerpt of the content instead of the full post.

To limit the number of posts shown on the page, log into your Wordpress site and navigate to Settings > Reading > Blog pages show at most, then set it to 10.

Limiting the amount of content in each post of the blog or category pages is a bit more complicated.

LIMIT THE SIZE OF EACH BLOGROLL POST

On the blogroll pages you don't want to show your entire post content. For example, when someone heads over to your page that lists all of your posts about fitness they want to see the list of posts that they can scan to determine which ones they may want to read. If each of the posts listed shows all of the content of the post then they aren't seeing a list. They are seeing a long page with all of the content from 10 posts. You don't want this.

To show excerpts instead of full posts on a blogroll page go to Settings > Reading > For each article in a feed show, then select Summary and click Save.

DISABLE PINGBACKS, TRACKBACKS AND COMMENTS

Pingbacks and trackbacks are automated communications between websites. A pingback is a notification sent from site A to site B indicating a link has been placed onto site A that points to site B. A trackback leaves a comment on site B on the page/post where the link is pointed to. Pingbacks and trackbacks take up resources including database records that are added for the comment trackbacks, and with time can become annoying. In particular, when your comments are flowing nicely and all of a sudden you see a ton of trackback comments that cloud the conversation.

If you don't want pingbacks and trackbacks taking up space in your database or comments then log into your Wordpress site and go to Settings >Discussions > Default article settings, then uncheck the top two checkboxes:

Default article settings	☑ Attempt to notify any blogs linked to from the article
	☑ Allow link notifications from other blogs (pingbacks and trackbacks) on new articles
	☑ Allow people to post comments on new articles
	(These settings may be overridden for individual articles.)

If you aren't interested in allowing comments to your blog posts at all then, uncheck the last checkbox also.

LIMIT THE NUMBER OF REVISIONS SAVED IN THE DATABASE

Each time you save content on your Wordpress site, a record is written to the database. For intensive editing sessions this can lead to 30, 60 or many more records stored. You can set the number of records that you allow to be stored by adding a line to the wp-config.php file in the root folder of your website. The line below is not included in the file by default, so I suggest you add it to the bottom of the file with an appropriate comment similar to the snippet below:

```
//21st added 7/7/20XX to limit the
number of revisions to 10
 define('WP_POST_REVISIONS', 10);
```

SET UP A CONTENT DELIVERY NETWORK (CDN), THE FINAL STEP IN WEBSITE OPTIMIZATION

I included this section because it is the final task in page load time optimization, but I don't want you to perform this task until you are completely done with the website, and it has been live for at least a few weeks. Because of this I have included a section towards the end of this book that explains more about how to add a content delivery network (CDN).

When you build a website, it resides on a web server that exists at a physical location and IP address somewhere out there in the ether of the Internet. As people visit your website the site content is fed from your web server to the visitor's computer, regardless of where the visitor exists. This means that your web server delivers content across the country and the world, depending on where the visitor is located.

Imagine that your company's website was served from many computers across the Internet instead of just one. When someone from Pascagoula, Mississippi visits your website, the content is delivered from a web server in Pascagoula. That is the concept behind a content delivery network (CDN). A CDN delivers your content optimally all across the world and provides a great performance boost. You can take advantage of this technology for free, or at minimal costs for higher-ended services.

Cloudflare is a great and reliable CDN. If you have taken my advice and hosted your Wordpress website at a hosting company that has a cPanel capability then you can usually install CloudFlare by clicking the Add-Ons or Upgrades menu items then follow the process. If you don't have this capability in your cPanel or control panel of your hosting company, then you can contact your hosting company to assist you, or go to CloudFlare.com directly. Create an account then use their instructions to set it up. I recommend starting with their free service unless you have special needs such as distributed denial of service (DDOS) protection or an SSL certificate (where your site is accessed by https:// yourdomain.com).

Why Optimize Wordpress If You're Going To Use A CDN?

You might think that jumping through the hoops of optimizing your website would be a lot of wasted time if you're going to ultimately use a CDN. There is a good reason for doing this. If you don't optimize first, then it is the same as the old saying of putting lipstick on a pig. It's still a pig. In our case, if you're loading a page that has eighty objects and takes fifteen seconds to load, then you add a CDN, you'll still be loading eighty objects. The page may then load in eight seconds instead of fifteen, but that is still too long. Current wisdom is that you don't want it to take any longer than four seconds to load else you risk a bounce – them just leaving the page before they ever saw it.

You want to reduce bounces. Bounce rate is one of the numbers tracked in Google Analytics. Bounce rate is the percentage of users that leave a site after visiting only one page. Of course, you want it to be a very low number.

If, however, you optimize the site first and reduce the number of page objects from eighty to forty-five and reduce native page load times down to three seconds, then when you add a CDN your pages might load in 1.5 seconds. That is much, much better for your site visitors and will increase conversions as well.

TASKS/PLUGINS FOR OPTIMUM AND SAFE WEBSITE PERFORMANCE

When you initially setup your site you need to make sure several important topics are covered like:

- Backups
- Security
- Editing
- SEO
- Content distribution

You want to immediately install plugins to backup your database, plugins, themes and uploaded images and media files. With all of those backups you can re-create your entire website. Also, if you are creating your site on a temporary URL before making it live, then you don't want to broadcast all of your new content to the search engines *yet.* If you do then all of that content will be credited to that temp URL address, and when you make it live on your real domain, it will be seen as duplicate content. You'll be penalized for that and it can take months to recover.

There are two important scenarios involved when you install your Wordpress website. Both are explained below. The benefits are maximizing your search engine rankings and activity, exploding your Internet content distribution, and avoiding potentially crippling search engine penalties.

The processes and tasks mentioned below make sure your efforts will all pay off and avoid problems.

SETUP WORDPRESS BACKUPS - A SAFETY NET

In the IT world, backups are always at the top of the requirements list. Backups save the day, and can possibly save the company. That is no exaggeration. I have seen catastrophes that could have easily been avoided had the company employees followed the simple backup procedures.

If your website gets hacked and you have backups of your database and all of your site files, then it is a simple matter to restore your site to its proper state. If this does happen then the next logical step would be to put preventions in place like changing passwords, stopping multiple login attempts from the same IP address and installing better security plugins. It is a simple effort to set up a secure website, and it is explained below.

There are many WordPress backup plugins. Covering all of them exhaustively is not only unnecessary, but unfruitful in the sense that so many of them would become outdated with time, so to even discuss them would be a waste of both of our times. I'm going to cover the ones that I think will stand the test of time and do the best job for you, as well as how to do it manually so you know and understand where the files are and what's important.

In case you're wondering if backing up your website is important and what it could mean to your company, here are a few failure modes of my personal experiences:

- **Disk failures** – yes, even hosting companies have hardware failures. If you back up regularly then you will be immune to this issue.

- **Network failures** – Hosting companies can and do have catastrophic network failures. In your case this means your website.

- **Failed optimization efforts** – If you try plugins that do wholesale changes to site components like images, javascript code or CSS code, then problems are possible. Make sure to back up all of your site's files and database before you make changes like this.

- **Hack attacks** – If your site is attacked and compromised by hackers for whatever reason, then you can quickly recover from your backups.

- **Failed to backup leads generated from the database** – I set up a client of mine with a custom database software application where all of their sales leads went into a database. I documented and trained their personnel and the owners on how to manage it all including backups, restores and testing the restores. Months later they changed the backup network drive from M to N. Even though my training included testing the restores regularly, they dropped this important detail. About six months after they changed the drive letter they called me to say that their database failed and they didn't have backups, and asked if I have some? The answer was no. They had to manually recover data from their paper records. The company never recovered completely from this catastrophic failure.

What Must Be Backed Up

In order to completely re-create your Wordpress installation you must back up the following:

1. Your Wordpress database

2. All of the files in the following folders. The base folder name will change depending on your hosting company:

base/public_html/wp-content/themes/

base/public_html/wp-content/plugins/

base/public_html/wp-content/uploads/

Below are the details of how to back up all of these site components.

Utilize Your Hosting Company's System Backups

Your hosting company usually provides complete system backups at no cost to you. I suggest logging into your cPanel going to the Files area, and there are two icons for it – Backups and Backup Wizard.

When you go to the Backup Wizard area you can download MySQL backups, Full Website backups, Full System backups and Email Forwarder backups. Email forwarders are virtual email addresses that just forward to another email address.

Do a backup of each of the above and store them locally. Do this periodically.

Backup Plugins to Automate Backups

What I am going to discuss and list here are a few free plugins that automate the process of backing up WordPress, ones that take a bit more expertise and elbow grease but are very reliable and paid plug-ins that you might also be interested in.

Automated Local and Off-Site Cloud Backups

BackWPUp - This plugin will automatically and on your schedule do backups of all of your files and the Wordpress database. It backs up them all to multiple places like Dropbox, an ftp site, Amazon S3, Microsoft Azure, Rackspace Cloud, SugarSync, email or another folder on your server. You can easily fine-tune the files it backs up. At the time of this writing it has over 500,000 installs with a 4/5 rating and was last updated five months ago.

When you read the negative reviews, many of them complain about not having a restore option. I don't see this as a problem. There are many ways to restore files and your database. You can restore your files with an FTP program, and you can restore your database using the cPanel tool phpMyAdmin. These are standard file and database management tools that you would ideally be familiar with.

BackWPUp also backs up important Wordpress files like .htaccess, wp-config.php and more critical system files.

Once activated BackWPUp takes you through a wizard where you configure the settings you desire for your backups.

Backup & Restore Dropbox is another possibility for automated backups, but you have to buy their Pro version to make them automatic. At the time of this writing it had 40,000+ installs with a 4.3/5 star rating and was updated four days ago.

WP-DBManager Database Backups - as mentioned above I recommend WP-DBManager to back up and optimize your Wordpress database. After installing and activating the plugin go to Database > DB Options > Automatic Scheduling, then make these setting changes:

Automatic Backing Up Of DB: 1 Days   Gzip: Yes

Automatic Optimizing Of DB: 2 Days

Automatic Repairing Of DB: 3 Days

You can set it up to email the database files to you regularly, or you can ftp the files down to your local computer manually as desired.

A Premium (Paid) Backup Tool

BackupBuddy has been around since 2010 and has more than 500,000 installs. It has a restore feature and also tools to migrate from one domain to another. I won't go into details of its features, but if you are always moving sites, or simply want one of the more robust solutions available, then you should check it out. It costs $80/year for one site, $100 for ten sites and up.

SECURITY PLUGINS FOR FREE AND ARMOR-PLATED WORDPRESS INSTALLATIONS

Limit Login Attempts

This plugin does just that, limits login attempts. This avoids a brute force attack where someone writes a script that attempts to login trying commonly (mis)used usernames and passwords like admin or administrator. Scripts like this try many login options like this, and Limit Login Attempts stops repeated login attempts by shutting off their IP address after a few attempts. It is simple to configure.

After installation you can leave the settings in the default position, and if you get a lot of emails indicating someone is attempting brute force breakins, then you can tighten up the settings at Settings > Limit Login Attempts

Wordfence Security

With over 15 million downloads, Wordfence is the only WordPress security plugin that can verify and repair your core, theme and plugin files, even if you don't have backups. Their website at https://www.wordfence.com/ interestingly shows a map of security attacks in real-time on Wordpress sites across the world. It has a firewall to stop brute-force attacks, a scanner, live traffic monitor and a premium version with password audits, country blocking, advanced comment spam filters and more.

Install and activate Wordfence Security then run a scan of your site and correct all problems it discovers.

Here are details of this process:

I. Go to the Wordfence > Scan menu and start your first security scan.

2. Once your first scan has completed, a list of security threats will appear. Go through them one by one to secure your site.

3. Visit the Wordfence Security > Options page to enter your email address, so that you can receive email security alerts.

4. Optionally change your security level or adjust the advanced options to set individual security scanning and protection options for your site.

5. Click the "Live Traffic" menu option to watch your site visitor activity in real-time.

Once configured, Wordfence will automatically secure and protect your Wordpress site through all of its activity.

WPMUDEV Defender

The developers of Wordpress have written an article on Hardening Wordpress. The Defender plugin from the people at WPMUDEV implements all of these recommendations. It is the only one on the market to do so, and as such you should consider buying this plugin if your website is mission-critical to your company. WPMUDEV is the most respected premier developer of Wordpress multiuser plugins and themes.

The cost of this plugin is the cost of a monthly subscription to all of the WPMUDEV products. With a two-week free trial the subscription costs $49/month. It includes 100+ plugins that all come with expert support and training. Again, if your site is mission-critical to your company I recommend that you at least browse the plugins available at WPMUDEV.

KEEP WORDPRESS, PLUGINS AND THEMES UP TO DATE – PLUG THE BIGGEST SECURITY HOLE

The most common reason that websites get compromised is that Wordpress itself or the plugins and themes are outdated. Hackers find out about vulnerabilities, and then they scan the Internet for sites to exploit.

You can avoid the problems due to outdated site components by always making sure your Wordpress, plugins and theme files are up to date. When you log into Wordpress you can navigate to Dashboard > Updates to see if there is anything that needs to be updated. Unless you have special circumstances, for example you have customized a theme or plugin and you don't want to wipe out your customizations, you should update everything that Wordpress indicates is outdated.

Below I discuss a couple tools that allow you to manage the updates and backups of multiple sites.

DELETE UNUSED PLUGINS AND THEMES

Because outdated code is an open door for website attacks, when you have plugins or themes that you aren't using then it is a good practice to always delete those you aren't using.

Tools To Manage Multiple Websites

In light of the importance of keeping your Wordpress, plugin and theme files up to date, if you have to manage multiple websites then this effort becomes unwieldy. Everyone has better things to do than logging into websites and updating software.

There are a couple great solutions to this problem. They both allow you to update all of your sites with a couple clicks. You can update all of Wordpress, plugins and themes at once.

Paid services also provide security scans of your site and many more features.

Both tools mentioned below require installing a Wordpress plugin that allows them to manage your updates remotely.

InfiniteWP

InfiniteWP is a tool with a free version that does all of the software updates mentioned above with a couple clicks. Security scans and many other add-ons can be purchased as separate add-ons such as uptime monitoring, broken link checker, staging to replicate your site for development and testing.

InfiniteWP is an installation on your web server as opposed to the cloud-based ManageWP which is discussed below. This means that you will need to create a database, install the application and configure it once installed. If you're not up to this then I recommend employing ManageWP.

You must install their Wordpress InfiniteWP – Client plugin to allow remote management of your site.

ManageWP

ManageWP is a paid service that charges by the services subscribed to and the number of sites that you are managing. Costs are very reasonable, and all levels include website security scans. Premium services include scheduled backups, multiple users, SEO analysis, traffic change alerts, cloning/website migration wizard and more.

If you aren't up to installing your own database and configuring it then subscribing to the very reasonably priced services at ManageWP is an easy decision to save you time in managing many websites.

You need to install the ManageWP Worker plugin for ManageWP to work.

SETTING UP WORDPRESS AS A LEAD GENERATION ENGINE

This is a very important topic since most websites exist *only* to generate leads then turn those prospects into paying customers, or to sell products directly.

Generating leads from your website can be accomplished many ways, and I'll describe a few that I have found to be most effective. This topic is much bigger than this and is the subject of many books in and of itself, so I can't exhaustively cover all of it in this book, but I will give you enough information to understand the topic and be proficient at producing high-quality leads and sales from your website. I'll list enough information to be able to research it further if you are so inclined, and multiple tools to get started immediately.

The concept goes as such: Create a compelling offer and present it to visitors on your website in exchange for their contact information when they complete a form. This is a business lead that you can follow-up on to see how you can help them – not to sell your products. That is the mistake most people make. They think sell, sell, sell, when they should be thinking of how they can help and benefit their site visitors the most and assist them in their path to meeting their own goals. *Your offerings must align with the most pressing needs of your ideal prospects,* and your communications with them must be the same. It's not about your services, it's about their pressing needs.

An example of an offer that aligns with prospects and gets the conversation started is the Software Development Checklist that I offer on my own website. It lists all factors that are critical in a custom database software project. It explains their significance and details about what you need to know about them. If you are interested in hiring someone to design and build a custom database software system for you, then making sure you consider all critical factors is important to project success. The last thing you want is to design and build a system only to realize after it is deployed that you missed important features like flexible reporting, security or multi-user capabilities. The information provided in the document points them in the right direction.

Getting someone to complete a form and download your free offer to become a business lead is both an art and a science. An art in the sense that it takes creativity to understand the burning questions and problems that your customers are seeking answers to. A science in that there is a methodical process that you should undertake to test, optimize and maximize your results.

Through the years, many people have asked me how to get traffic to their website, and employed me to do it. My first question is: How many conversions do you currently get? The answer is usually zilch. I then explain that getting more traffic isn't going to fix that. Converting existing website visitors is where they need to start. Many of these companies provide big-ticket services, so even a handful of real leads a month would make a difference to them. If their website got 1,000 visitors a month that converted at 10%, and 10% of those leads converted into paying customers then they'd have 10 new customers a month. Once you have achieved conversion and sales rates like this, it is time to bring in more traffic. Not before.

To maximize your websites ability to generate leads do the following:

1. Brainstorm the problems of your ideal customers/ prospects and solutions to each. This should be straightforward since you are in the business of solving those problems.

2. Put together a list of offers that you can present to those ideal prospects that solve their problems. Some examples:

   A. Free consultations

   B. Free downloadable white papers

   C. Tickets to the football game

D. One free month of your services

E. One free month of your services with one (or two or three) paid

F. Free Trials so they can take your product for a test drive

G. A free eBook, audio or print version of the book you wrote

H. A free copy of your mobile app

I. One free drink on their next visit

J. 50% off your first purchase

K. A free eBook for joining your list

You get the point.

3. Gather associated material to test on the landing pages of your website. Landing page are where you place and test your offers. The list of materials would include (in priority order of what is most likely to sway your conversions – the stronger the material the higher the conversion):

A. The offers themselves

B. Description of the offer

C. List of benefits

D. List of features

E. Ultra-relevant images – they are all the difference, so be meticulous in gathering the right ones to use and test on your landing page. Stock photos will get you the least mileage. Think about using photos of:

I. The quality that separates you and your products and services from the competition. This is big since most people are very visual. Think about how you can visually express the difference your company makes.

II. Results

III. Your product being used by happy customers

IV. Your real customers interacting with you and your team

V. Strategy sessions

F. Headings

G. Subheadings

4. Build a landing page and test all of the material above. There are plugins and third party products and services to do all of this. More on landing pages below.

5. Place calls to action in all of the relevant pages of your website that point to your landing page. What is a call to action you ask? Read below.

6. Optimize your landing page until your conversion rates are above 10%. If you see great strides in your conversions then don't stop testing. Continue until they start to plateau.

7. Bring traffic to your landing page using pay-per-click (PPC) advertising.

Specialized Landing Pages To Drive Conversions for Your Main Products/Services

As explained above, landing pages are all about increasing your website conversions and turn website visitors into paying customers. A landing page is a special purpose page that exists *only* to convert visitors into leads, grab their contact information and thereby add them to your email list so you can continue to correspond with them. It consists of multiple elements including visual, textual and offers (or lead magnets). It is then up to you to nourish that lead and turn them into a paying customer.

After you have optimized your landing pages, you'll place calls to action on your website to draw site visitors to each of the landing pages you have optimized. This is detailed in the Calls to Action (CTA) section below.

Landing pages can be assembled manually by just entering content into Wordpress, or you can use third-party tools and plugins to assist you in this effort. Once assembled you'll need to test and optimize to determine what combination of content converts at the highest rates. You should continue this testing ad infinitum. In the case of the customer I mentioned above, of you are getting 300 leads a month at a value of $300,000, then why wouldn't you be interested in increasing that by 10% for an extra website leads value of $30,000? The cost of optimization is incremental compared to the added value of leads and sales due to your optimized landing pages. *As you optimize the landing pages and increase conversion rates they become valuable company assets.*

Before creating a landing page you need to gather the content about your products and services that you'll place onto the page(s) that you'll be testing. A good place to start in this effort is to see what *your competitors* are doing on their landing pages. What are their offers? What imagery and benefits are they using? Think of this effort as defining your target. If you don't learn the current state of the product or service offerings in your industry are then you may miss something important. I'd venture to say that you will *probably* miss something *very* important if you don't research your competition. Once you place everything onto the table and see what your competitors are offering and how they're going about it then you can craft a plan to do it better. You would simply never know the better plan unless you have done at least some level of competitive analysis.

Competitive Analysis Tools To Smoke Your Competitors

Go to your competitor's website and see how their product/service content and calls to action are positioned. Go to SpuFu and see what text ads they are running and what keywords they are buying. At Follow.net you can see what banner ads they are running. It is worth the $79 for SpyFu and $37 for Follow.net for a month of each of those services while you do this research. Do this for each of your competitors and tally all of the information in a spreadsheet for quick reference. Now you have more information about how to position your own products on a landing page. Using the tools at WhatRunsWhere will also give you a comprehensive look at the landscape of what your competitors are doing online. It will show you the ads they are running, what ads are working the best and where the ads are running. It assists you in finding new sites to place your ads with confidence, and immediately increases your click through rates.

Once you have your road partially mapped out, assemble multiple versions of all of the following information about your own products/services:

- Your offers and lead-magnets
- Benefits – make a complete list then prioritize them
- Headlines
- Sub-Headlines
- Features – just like benefits, make a complete list
- Images – ideally stay away from stock photos
- Descriptions and written content – craft the essential and most important attributes of your product or service

Split Testing and Multivariate Testing Tools
to Achieve 50% Conversion Rates

Once you have gathered all of the content above you will assemble all of it into landing pages that you'll test and optimize. The testing phase will either involve split (also known as A/B) testing or multivariate testing. Split testing involves testing one option against another, whereas multivariate testing serves and tests multiple page components at once. What you want to ultimately end up with is the combination of page objects that together result in more conversions. If you split test then you can first test your offer and after you have determined the offer that results in the statistically significant best option, then you test the next component like the benefits. In this fashion you move through all of your landing page components until all have been tested. This process can result in improvement of your conversion rates from maybe 1% or 2% to 10%, 20% and higher. I have run multiple tests that have resulted in over 50% conversion rates, so this is truly a game changer.

Multivariate testing involves testing multiple components on the page at once. To do this you need a lot of traffic. You can buy it from places like Google Adwords advertising. Google has the most search engine traffic out there and you can target it to your specific campaign needs. You can also obviously send Adwords traffic to your pages if you are split testing.

A simple plugin that you can use for split testing pages is the Simple Page Tester. It allows you to build one page, clone it, then run and monitor your test with the built-in analytics. Conversion tracking only comes with the Premium version with a standard license for your own sites at $59.

As you do your A/B testing you'll need to determine when one of your options has statistically outscored the other, so you can drop that test and move on to the next. I use Perry Marshall's SplitTester tool to do this manually. It determines which ad is performing better than the other by entering the number of clicks and the click-through-rate (CTR) of both of your ads. Once you enter that it will tell you which ad is better than the other along with a degree of statistical certainty. You can switch clicks and click-through-rates with conversions and conversion rates to get the same determination for your conversions. If your test currently shows one option with a 70% chance of being better than the other then you need to keep testing. If one option has a 99% chance of being better than the other then you should end the test, drop the losing content and replace it with another. If this 99% chance was hit last week and you are paying for the traffic to the page then you've wasted a weeks worth of money on the test traffic. You need to monitor your results often. I usually make determinations at the 90% level.

If you want do multivariate testing and you have committed to the cost of bringing in the traffic using online advertising or other high-traffic means then Visual Website Optimizer is a great tool that is simple to use. Its built in analytics is all you need to determine what *combination* of page content converts the best.

3rd Party Landing Page Services That Simplify and Automate the CRO Process

There are many third party landing page services that you can use that will immediately increase your efficiency and speed up your conversion rate optimization (CRO) efforts. They have templates that have proven to convert at the highest levels – and they know because they also run the analytics on those pages that prove it. Tools like LeadPages get you up to speed quickly, have a split testing built in and integrate seamlessly with Wordpress. Once you create your landing page you can just select it in Wordpress (after installing their plugin) and run it on your own site, which is advisable since it is your company that is asking for their contact information.

The templates at LeadPages have had millions of visitors interact with them. They know what templates work best, and you have direct access to them.

See this list of landing page vendors and resources in my blog post at 21stsoft.com. There are free Wordpress plugins, other vendors like LeadPages and resources to improve and learn about landing pages that you can use in your efforts to improve website conversions.

Effective Calls to Action (CTA) Multiply Conversion Rates

After you have created and optimized landing pages then you need to direct your website traffic to them. Calls to action accomplish this. A call to action is a visual object on your page that catches the eye of the visitor and causes them to click through to the landing page with your offer. A call to action must accomplish both of the above or it has failed its job. The "action" part of it is something like download a document or start a free trial now. An effective call to action can make a huge difference in the results you get from your website.

I placed calls to action on one of my client sites and the daily leads we got went from one to two leads per day to ten to eighteen per day. Those leads are worth $1,000 to $2,000 each, so the difference to the client was dramatic. The carefully designed and placed calls to action on the site made a massive difference in this customers sales.

Some call to action guidelines:

- Use verbs to make your action clear, understandable and straightforward.

- Highlight a strong offer.

- Make it relevant. Offering a free coffee on your next visit isn't relevant to someone that lives across the country.

- Make the CTA visually stand out from the rest of the page content. Stand back from your screen and if it can't be separated and recognized from a distance as a unique object on the page then change the design to make it stand out more. If most objects on the page are square then make it round. If the site uses pastel colors then use bold colors in your CTA that contrast with the rest of the objects on the page.
- Make use of whitespace in the CTA design.

Here are a few examples of great calls to action:

From http://well.org, a wellness company:

From http://blog.hubspot.com/marketing/great-call-to-action-examples:

A retargeting ad from online analytics and reporting company http://spyfu.com:

This ad was served to me on another site after I visited SpyFu.com. It's called ad retargeting. The ads follow you around the Internet and are the reason behind the "creepy" factor that people talk about. It ends up that, when done correctly and when you don't overdo it, ad retargeting can be a very effective form of online advertising.

From the woodworking equipment and training company http://roclker.com/retail/stores/

Luxury portable restrooms company Royal Restrooms at https://royalrestrooms.com:

Autoresponders Communicate With Your Prospects

After you bring people to your landing pages and have them convert into business leads and prospects, you need to close the deal. Autoresponders assist in this effort. An autoresponder is a pre-written series of emails that are sent to each new subscriber to your email list. These emails introduce your company and warm up your prospect to understanding the benefits of working with you.

The biggest advantage of autoresponders is that you only have to write your email content once, then every time someone signs up for your email list they receive the entire email sequence. These emails can play a critical part of the sales funnel that starts with someone completing a form on your site.

Here are some examples of what you can do to nourish a relationship with the people who join your list, so they feel comfortable engaging with you and spending their money with your company:

- Introduce them to your tech support leader with a photo (to make it more personal) and a direct phone number.

- Instruct then on how to get started with the products/services/ideas they just purchased or downloaded.

- Introduce the benefits of the products they have already shown an interest in.

- Extend the information in the document they downloaded when they completed the form on your site.

- Curate some relevant articles from other companies that highlight topics of interest to them. Yes, sending them information that others have created is appropriate. It instills an element of trust and demonstrates that you are serious in helping them any way you can.

- Introduce them to the benefits of your professional upgraded suite of products.

- Give them advance notice of early bird pricing that goes up after a certain date.

- Send them notifications of important industry or company events.

If your autoresponder does its job, then people will be calling you at specific junctures inquiring about how you can help them.

There are many popular autoresponder services available out there and I have used most of them. The top services include MailChimp, Aweber, GetResponse, Constant Contact and iContact.

Simple Wordpress Website Forms with An Autoresponder

The autoresponders described above are used to correspond with people who have *given you permission to communicate with them.* If you just put them on your list and start sending them emails, then they'll just unsubscribe, and you will have wasted your efforts. Not only that, if you send people spam emails without their permission you may be breaking the laws of the US CAN-SPAM act of 2003 which can get you into a lot of trouble. Canadian laws are more strict that the US version, so before you start sending people unsolicited emails make sure you are compliant with the email laws of your country.

Sometimes you just want people to either call you or complete a form, and in these cases a simple Wordpress form tool and plugin will work. You don't want to lose their contact information, so you need to set up your forms to save all form completions and contact information to a database.

I'll mention a few popular form plugins that you can use and give you some details about a free one that I have used for years. Gravity forms has been around a long time, but it costs $39 at the time of this writing. Since Jetpack is installed by default, then using their Wordpress Contact Form is a viable option. You might also consider Very Simple Contact Form.

The plugin I have used for years is Contact Form 7. It has great flexibility in what fields you can have in your forms like text fields, checkboxes, big textarea boxes, dropdowns, radio buttons and even CAPTCHA boxes and quizzes to avoid spam. Contact Form 7 Allows you to create forms for the landing pages or sidebars by copying and pasting a shortcode where you want the form.

Once you install and activate the plugin go to the Contact menu item in Wordpress and in the Form tab either use their default form or modify the default code to set up a customized form. You can add different fields by clicking on the buttons that say checkboxes, text, email, etc. Next click the Mail tab to customize the emails that go out when someone completes the form. Then, to install the form on your sidebar or page/pos,t place the Wordpress shortcode provided into the HTML tab. It will look something like this:

```
[contact-form-7 id="777"
title="Contact Us Form"]
```

Optional Redirect To A Different Page After Form Completion

If you need to redirect to a different page after a form completion for reasons of maybe tracking conversions, then you can add code similar to this in the Additional Settings tab of the Contact Forms page:

```
on_sent_ok: "location = 'http://
yourdomain.com/thank-you/';"
```

If you're doing PPC advertising and want to track conversions then this is also the page where you'll need to install your conversion code that Google gives you.

CRM/Marketing Automation – The Next Level Up

When you have outgrown your autoresponders listed above for various reasons like the number of people in your list, then your next logical step up is to use customer relationship management (CRM), or marketing automation software. It costs hundreds to thousands of dollars per month instead of tens to hundreds, but it is the next logical step in your online marketing efforts. With these powerful tools you can:

- Manage hundreds of thousands of emails in your lists.

- Visually map out and track the numbers for your marketing campaigns in terms of email to landing pages to sales.

- Track the success of every step of your sales funnels, so you can see the weakest points of your funnel and constantly improve them to increase your overall conversion rates.

- Send behavioral-based emails.

- Send shopping cart abandonment emails when people leave your cart.

A few marketing automation tools you should consider are Infusionsoft, Ontraport and SharpSpring. A couple CRM systems to consider are HubSpot (which also does marketing automation), Netsuite and SalesForce. For a low-cost CRM solution you can check out Zoho, or one of the many open source CRM or marketing automation (Google searches) solutions.

Roll Out the Content That You Have Tested and Proven To Convert the Best

Now that you have tested your landing pages with PPC advertising and determined what content works the best, it's time to roll out.

If you were bringing traffic to your landing pages via Google Adwords and you have been tracking conversions and optimizing your landing pages as described above, then you have learned the following:

1. What keywords converted the best?

2. What ads drew the most clicks and converted the best?

3. What combinations of landing page content converted the best?

These literally golden nuggets of information that can change your company if you do the next steps correctly, so why wouldn't you? You now know what works – to the hundredth. If you bring traffic in from other channels, then you can expect better results than if you had come up with content from out of the blue, or from what just makes sense at the time. This can separate you from your competition and pull in front of them to gain an insurmountable lead that they'll be hard-pressed to overcome.

The next step is to take what worked and create content on your website around it. Drop the keywords in your PPC campaign that *aren't* working, add more budget to what *is* working then roll out your best content to other ad networks.

Here's how you go about it:

1. Group your highest converting keywords into logical groups that will be used as the basis for future website content.

2. Form themes around them associated with solutions to your customer's problems and write a few series of blog posts using the grouped keywords.

3. Use the ad content that drew the most clicks and converted the best, and variations of it in the titles and meta-descriptions of your sites pages and posts.

4. Create social media posts and tweets using the top keywords in #hashtags and a URL that points to the posts you created above.

5. Drop the keywords in your ad campaign that aren't producing and add that budget to the keywords that are bringing in the most conversions. Think 80/20, the Pareto principle. Keep the top 20% most successful keywords and drop the 80% that aren't producing. Your cost per lead will immediately go way down.

6. Take the same keywords and ads and start running them in other PPC ad networks like Bing, Yahoo and maybe second-tier networks like Bing, Yahoo, 7Search, Propel Media or Advertise.com.

7. Buy keyword-based traffic from other sources. I use a proprietary platform that pops up a banner at the top of the browser when the keywords I pay for are searched on. The advantage of using this type of advertising is that you don't have to manage a campaign. You create the banner, put the keyword and let it run. My clients and my own companies have bought hundreds of keywords using this platform. It looks like this:

These tasks essentially map out what content you'll be writing and what marketing and advertising you can be doing for months. The results you achieve are based on what works. Rolling out effective content to multiple channels is ultimately what will make you successful online.

THE MOST POWERFUL AND VERSATILE SEO PLUGIN YOU CAN GET - YOAST SEO

Out of the box Wordpress has many features that are great for SEO like permalinks (SEO-friendly URLS) and tags, but it is neither perfect nor complete. Using the Yoast SEO plugin will add a lot of features that enhance your website's SEO and correct problems of out-of-the-box Wordpress. Many SEO plugins have been developed through the years, but

Yoast SEO is the best one to ever hit the Wordpress plugins marketplace. It is one of the most downloaded Wordpress plugins.

Yoast SEO plugin covers the following bases for you:

- Page/post SEO optimization and readability tools.

- Creates XML Sitemaps.

- SEO Title and Meta-Description editors that have a red warning when the field is too long.

- Creates default titles and meta-descriptions for pages where you don't submit these fields. This is good for pages like tags, categories and author pages that Wordpress creates automatically and in general you don't edit. You can, but most people don't. Without this feature these pages would be left without the title and description and produce SEO errors as far as the search engines are concerned.

- Capability to import and export SEO plugin settings.

- Specify information to optimally submit your Wordpress posts to each of the top social media sites.

- Google Search Console report information.

- Tools to edit your .htaccess file and robots.txt files.

Once Yoast SEO is installed and activated, go to SEO > XML Sitemaps then make the following setting changes:

General Tab

XML sitemap functionality: Enabled

User Sitemap Tab

User Sitemap > Author / user sitemap > Disabled

Post Types Tab

Enable Posts, Pages and media because images can be found in Google also.

Taxonomies Tab

Due to duplicate content issues and Google penalties for it, I suggest that you add tags to your sitemap and exclude categories. This is why I recommended disabling the author / user sitemap above. On on this tab, set Tags to In sitemap and Categories to Not in sitemap.

Next go to SEO > Social and add your social media URLs and Open Graph info for Facebook, Twitter, Pinterest and Google+.

You can also add a custom header and footer for your RSS feeds. You can do that at SEO > Advanced > RSS.

SITE PERFORMANCE PLUGIN TO SPEED UP PAGE LOAD TIMES

Autoptimize https://wordpress.org/plugins/autoptimize/ is a plugin that reduces file sizes and file count by minimizing and combining them. The end result is that many files are reduced dramatically in size and they're combined with others resulting in fewer http requests and faster page load times.

Before you run this plugin, or any plugin that is going to make wholesale changes to your site, make sure to backup all of the site files (plugins, themes, uploads and the root folder files) so you can use them in case of total failure. After you activate it you need to check all of the functional parts of your pages (sliders, menus, forms, etc.) to make sure they all work after the optimization effort. If not then tweak the settings or uncheck the entire section that is causing the problem. For example, if the styling is not right then tweak the CSS settings, and if you lose functionality of movable objects on the site, tweak the Javascript section by checking/unchecking the options.

It may take some experimentation on your part, but it is fairly simple to configure this plugin as compared to other optimization and cache plugins I have used. One nice thing about this one is that if you lose some functionality after enabling it you can disable specific sections of it and get the functionality back. I optimized a site once with W3 Total Cache and it broke the site. I had no recourse other than to restore from backup files. Needless to say, it was annoying at the very least.

Before running Autoptimize I baselined with these results at http://webpagetest.org:

	Load Time	First Byte	Start Render	Speed Index	DOM Elements	Document Complete			Fully Loaded		
						Time	Requests	Bytes In	Time	Requests	Bytes In	Cost
First View	4.870s	1.448s	2.096s	2585	622	4.870s	69	739 KB	7.032s	71	768 KB	$$—
Repeat View	0.485s	0.329s	0.697s	712	620	0.485s	3	8 KB	1.107s	6	50 KB	

These are the results after configuring Autoptimize:

	Load Time	First Byte	Start Render	Speed Index	DOM Elements	Document Complete			Fully Loaded		
						Time	Requests	Bytes In	Time	Requests	Bytes In	Cost
First View	3.497s	1.682s	2.088s	3018	590	3.497s	36	552 KB	6.718s	55	755 KB	$$—
Repeat View	0.336s	0.221s	0.497s	511	589	0.336s	2	8 KB	0.710s	6	50 KB	

The Document Complete number of requests was reduced from 69 to 36, and the load time for the First View improved by 1.373 seconds, a 28% improvement in page load time. That's significant.

I optimized HTML, Javascript and CSS. The only tweak I had to make was to add jquery.js to the "Exclude scripts from Autoptimize" section. When it optimized jquery.js the image slider on my home page failed, and that fixed it.

A quick 28% improvement page load time with Autoptimize. That's always nice.

ADD PAGE/POST TITLE LINK TO FOOTER AREA

This is a trick I learned a few years back that increases the relevance of your website content. It places a link in the footer of every page and post of your site that points to your home page with the text in the link the same as the title of that particular page. For example, if the title of your post is

"7 Ways To Achieve Local SEO Rankings" then there will be a text link at the bottom of the post with that as the anchor text that points to your home page which increases the relevance of those words for your website. Think about it. Each post that you write will have a link with that post's title that points to your home page. It tells the search engines that that particular post is relevant to the website in general because the link points to the home page.

To make this possible you need to install two sets of code – one goes into your functions.php to create the shortcode, and the other goes into the footer area of your website.

Add this code to your functions.php file in the /themes/ yourtheme/ folder of your website.

```
// This shortcode returns the page/
post title:
// [mytitle]
function myshortcode_title () {
    return get_the_title();
}
add_shortcode('mytitle',
'myshortcode_title');
```

Place this code into the footer area of your website:

```
<a href="http://yourdomain.com"
title="[mytitle]">[mytitle]</a>
```

Of course, change yourdomain.com to your own domain.

ACTIONS TO TAKE/PLUGINS TO INSTALL *JUST BEFORE* SITE LAUNCH

This section assumes all content has been completed and the site is ready to launch. Complete the following tasks to launch the website.

GOOGLE SEARCH CONSOLE URL SETTING

You need to set your preferred domain at Google Search Console. I'm not going to step you through the details of registering at Google Search Console, but I'll say that you create your account then you have to verify ownership of your site. You can do this by uploading a file to the root folder of your website, by adding meta-tags to your pages or other means. Once you have completed this then continue with the instructions below.

So, you have registered your site and verified it. Next, in Search Console click the gear icon at the top-right and select Site Settings > Preferred domain. If it is already set to what you have set in Wordpress then leave it. If not then set it to your desired method of site access, either with or without the www at the front-end of your site URL and with or without the secure https reference. This will give full credit to your website for links that point to your pages that have the www in them as well as those that don't.

Canonical

A canonical URL tag is a meta-tag that is placed into the <head></head> area of your web pages. It is similar to a 301 redirect in that it passes the SEO juice of all links to the designated URL. When search engines created the canonical tag it was hailed by Rand Fishkin at MOZ as "one of the biggest advancements in SEO practices since sitemaps". The canonical tag, however, *is not a 301 redirect.* It is just a designator giving search engines guidance on where to place SEO value for a page.

An example canonical tag would be:

```
<link rel="canonical" href="https://
yourdomain.com/blog/" />
```

This means that all links that point to this page, regardless of having www or index.php or index.html or any other variation of the URL in them will pass all SEO juice to the https://yourdomain.com/blog/ URL.

To implement canonical tags on your site simply install and activate the Yoast SEO plugin. There are no settings to change, and it will automatically add the canonical tag to the header of all of your site pages. If for some reason you need to change the default canonical URL of a page/post you can change it on the individual page/post at Yoast SEO Settings > Advanced (gear icon).

INSTALL GOOGLE ANALYTICS

I recommend using Google Analytics to track visitor's activity on your website. It is free, configurable and easy to install. Most themes come with a Header box that you can install the code into, and if not then you can install a plugin to give you the capability to install the Google Analytics code. I'm intentionally leaving out the option that requires coding, but I'll say that all Wordpress themes come with a header.php file and if you are courageous then you can jump in and edit your theme files directly.

To get started at Google Analytics, go to http://google.com/analytics and create an account for your website. Then, to find the code you need to install on your site, log into your Google Analytics account then go to Admin > Property > Tracking Info > Tracking Code. The analytics code Google provides you is in the javascript language. In most cases you want to install javascript code in the footer of your pages. Google analytics is an exception. In order to use tagging properly you need to install it between the <head></head> tags in your theme.

Your theme will have special areas to install this code, for example at Theme Options > Header > Integration, but it is different for each theme, so I can't tell you where it is in your theme.

You might want to try the Monster Insights plugin at https://www.monsterinsights.com/ that has over 11 million downloads and is the most popular Google Analytics plugin available.

Customized Dashboards For Tracking Sales, SEO, Mobile, Adwords, Social Media, Affiliate Performance...

Google Analytics has a lot of ways to slice and dice the information they track about your website visitors. It can be intimidating. I suggest watching a few YouTube videos to get a quick leg up on it. Just go to YouTube.com and do a search for Google analytics. There are many that are 5 – 60 minutes in length with tens or hundreds of thousands of views.

A great feature of Google Analytics is their dashboards. Once you're familiar with it you can set it up for your own specific purposes. For example, if you're interested in your SEO performance you can install an SEO dashboard. Same with mobile, sales, social media, your Adwords campaigns, affiliate performance or many more specific purposes.

To see many customized dashboards that you can install for free go to http://www.dashboardjunkie.com/. Click on a dashboard of interest to you, click the button to install this dashboard, then log into your Google Analytics account to select the website and add this dashboard to that account. After installation go to Dashboards > Private > The dashboard you just installed. You'll see the information grouped nicely in chart and table formats for the specific purpose of the dashboard. You can then run the mouse over each item, click the edit pencil then customize the presentation of the data.

INSTALL/CONFIGURE PLUGINS - THE WORDPRESS SECRET SAUCE

Comment Spam Manager

Akismet is a free crowdsourcing plugin that monitors the comments placed onto your site and marks them as spam if many others have done the same for this commenter. If you strive to get a lot of comments on your posts then this plugin will save you a ton of time by sorting out the real comments from the spam.

You have to create an account at Akismet then grab their API key and insert it into your site to register the plugin, but this effort only takes a few minutes.

Related Posts Plugin

A related posts plugin is a good idea for your site if you want people to engage with your content and dig further into your articles. Site engagement is a Google organic SEO ranking factor, so having visitors dig deeper into your content not only accomplishes your branding goals, but gets you higher search engine rankings. There are many related posts plugins, and I'll talk about the one I have used for years.

Yet Another Related posts Plugin (YARPP) is a popular plugin that has over 300,000 active installs and provides a widget that you place onto your sidebar containing posts that are related to the post your visitor is reading. It also adds a Related posts section to the bottom of your posts and RSS feed. YARPP coerces people into digging further into your content after they have read a post that they find interesting.

The plugin can be tweaked in terms of what posts you want to include in their algorithm for what is related and the display options. Make sure to check the Display Options box for "Display related posts in feeds?"

If you have a large site then buying the pro version will offload the heavy work to their servers. Keep in mind that managed Wordpress hosting sites like WPEngine will block it, but otherwise you're Ok to get the pro version.

Wordpress Cache Plugin

One of the easiest and most important usability and SEO capabilities you can add to your website is caching (pronounced cashing). Caching is the process of storing pre-processed page content then serving it to visitors if the content hasn't changed. This saves a lot of unnecessary server processing and resources, and speeds up your page load times.

WP Super Cache is a great Wordpress cache management plugin. When a page is requested from a visitor's browser, it is delivered from your web server, and there are a lot of moving parts to make that happen. Several sets of software, CPU and memory resources, database processing and more are involved. You can see them in the diagram in the "Get a Hosting Account" section above. The web server has to execute a lot of code, retrieve content from the database then execute more code to assemble and send it across the Internet to your browser. A caching plugin will check to see if that page has been requested before, and if so, and if the page exists in the cache, then the content is served as a static cache file instead of having to go through all of the processing and database communications. This speeds up your page load times considerably which is a usability (nobody wants to wait forever for a page to load) as well as an SEO benefit – Google awards you with higher rankings for fast page load times, and your site visitors are happy because your pages load quickly.

Do the following after installing and activating WP Super Cache:

1. Click Settings > WP Super Cache.

2. Click onto the Advanced tab.

3. Check box next to "Cache hits to this website."

4. Select the button next to "Use mod_rewrite to serve cache files."

5. Check the box next to "Compress Pages."

6. Check the box next to "304 Not Modified browser caching."

7. Check the box next to "Don't cache pages for known users."

"Cache rebuild" & "Extra homepage checks" should already be checked, leave them that way.

8. Select "Update Status" button. Then, scroll down and select "Update Mod_Rewrite Rules" in the yellow box.

9. Scroll down to "Expiry Time & Garbage Collection" and enter "3600" in the box, then select "Change Expiration."

10. Scroll down, remove entries in "Rejected User Agents" and select "Save UA Strings."

After you have optimized the site then de-activate WP Super Cache and re-activate it when you launch the site, because otherwise as you're building content, each time you make a change to the site you have to clear the cache from this plugin.

Broken Link Checker

Installing and activating the Broken Link Checker plugin will place a new section on the Wordpress Dashboard page that lists all broken links on the site. You need to fix all of the ones that are links in your content by pointing them to an appropriate URL, and if there are any external, outgoing links in comments then just delete them. It also displays broken links in your content with a ~~strikethrough~~.

Broken links will incur Google penalties so this is another important SEO tool to embrace..

I recommend de-activating it after you have fixed all of the internal broken links on your site, then activating it periodically to make sure there are no broken links.

Visitor Sitemap

The DDSiteMapGen plugin creates a visitor sitemap that lists all of the pages and posts on your site. Once installed and activated you add it to a page with one line of code. Just create a page named sitemap, then add this code into the Text tab of the page:

```
<!-- ddsitemapgen -->
```

To configure it go to Settings > DDSitemapGen. There are a few simple settings. Set them to your preferences then save your changes.

The order of the pages in your site, typically Contact Us, About Us, Privacy Policy, etc. are arranged by the Order field of the page. To change the order of the pages that appear in the Sitemap page, do the following:

1. Open a tab to the sitemap page on the site, so you can refresh it periodically to see the results of the page re-ordering you are doing.

2. Login to your Wordpress account then click the menu items Pages > Pages.

3. Run the mouse over the page you want to order and click the Quick Edit link under the page title.

4. Select the parent page if needed then add the order

you want the page to appear on the Sitemap page. If you use one of the existing pages as a parent, then the menu item will appear as a sub-menu to that page. If you select Main Page (no parent) then this page will appear as a left-most page and not indented under a parent page on the sitemap page.

5. To keep a page *off of the menu* go to Pages > Pages and run the mouse over the title of the page you don't want on the sitemap page. At the bottom of your browser screen you'll see the URL of that page and part of it will have post=xxxx. Take note of the post id number, go to Settings > DDSiteMapGen, enter it into the Exclusions > Excluded Pages box then save your changes.

Structured Data and Rich Snippet Plugins to Separate You From Your Competition in the SERP

The HTML (and XHTML) and CSS that make up the content of web pages ruled the Internet for years. Then Google wanted more. They wanted a way to differentiate between content and *data*. Content might be the blog post you just wrote about a fishing technique and your favorite place to fish (as if), or how to install an alternator on a 1965 Ford Galaxie 500 (Love those old classics. I used to have one of these.):

Photo courtesy: https://www.shannons.com.au

Data might be your company's name, address and phone number or a review of your company or product. It can be a recipe, your restaurant's menu or many other data items specific to businesses. You can see information about a lot of the types of data that has been formalized at http://schema.org/docs/schemas.html.

The benefit of using structured data on your website is that *Google will show this data on their search engine results page (SERP)*. See this example of a normal SERP listing without any structured data involved:

> El Tejado Menu | Mexican Cuisine | Mexican Restaurant | Denver, CO
> www.eltejadodenver.com/menu/398653
> Browse El Tejado's Menu. Breakfast, lunch, and dinner. Mexican cuisine. Appetizers. Hot seafood soup. Burgers. Chicken. Steak. Desserts. Call 303-722-3987.

Standard, and has been for years. See this example of how Bing shows a recipe with structured data:

> **Chicken** Parmigiana **Recipe** : Bobby Flay : **Food Network**
> www.foodnetwork.com/recipes/bobby-flay/chicken-parmigiana-recipe.html
> By Bobby Flay · Difficulty: Intermediate · 5 steps · 1 hr 15 mins
>
> | Overview | Ingredients | Steps | Related |
>
> Total Time: 1 hr 15 min. Yield: 4 servings. Bobby Flay goes Italian with his recipe for mouthwatering Chicken Parmigiana, from Boy Meets Grill on Food Network. Try panko breadcrumbs for a lighter crust. You can also find 1000s of Food Network's best recipes from top chefs, shows and experts. And watch videos demonstrating recipe prep and cooking techniques.
>
> See more on www.foodnetwork.com

Note the multiple tabs that show the details of the recipe, and also note that *this is on the search engine results page, not the Food Network website.*

Here is an example of how Google shows the structured data/rich snippets information. This is a screenshot of the results for a search for best chicken parmesan recipe from the top:

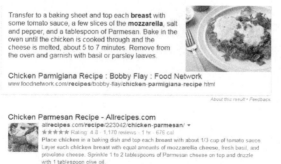

The second listing shows the average star rating of the recipe from allrecipes.com along with the number of reviews and the calories of the recipe and an excerpt from the recipe. Clearly this is better than the El Tejado listing at the top of this section. (FYI, El Tejado is my favorite Mexican restaurant in Denver) The first Google listing for Chicken Parmesan is emphasized by placing the recipe in the enlarged box at the top with a larger photo and an excerpt from the recipe *that Google thinks will draw your click*. That's how they operate. So, why is there not a star rating in the top listing? I just tested it and Google isn't placing the star ratings in that box for anyone. Still, I suspect that that top listing draws the most clicks.

You can test your own structured data using the Google tool at https://search.google.com/structured-data/testing-tool.

All of this can and will change in the future, but like I have said before, all of your company and website online strategies and activities should be soundly based on your own business goals and not *only* based on Google rankings.

Many companies through the years have made the mistake of chasing Google's organic search ranking algorithm, so they can get top organic rankings for their keywords, and many died when Google changed the same algorithm. Literally died. They pursued the trick of the day that achieved temporary rankings, then got dumped from Google's database when Google determined that these tactics weren't in the best interest of their searching customers.

My advice to you is to do what is best for your company and to not focus solely on your Google rankings. Focus on the quality of your own products and services. Focus on the quality of your presentation. Embrace the technologies that you feel will continue, and will take your company into the future, integrate them into your website and company processes then you'll always be standing on more solid ground.

So, now you see that it is in your best interest to place rich data onto your website to separate your company's products and services from your competitor's content on the Internet. Rich snippets are all about appropriately *coding* your website's most important data and information. The good news is that there are plugins that do the code for you. They make integration easy, write the code for you and ensure that your structured data content and code is compliant with the latest standards.

There are Wordpress plugins that make it simple for you to accomplish this, and the ones I recommend here will work for most businesses.

I. Rich Reviews – a free shortcode-based plugin where you add a few shortcodes to your pages/posts to add star ratings, the text of the reviews and forms for your site visitors to add their reviews. You have the option to automatically approve the reviews or to have them approved by an administrator. Or example, here is the Wordpress shortcode that lists the reviews:

```
[RICH_REVIEWS_SNIPPET category="post"]
```

and here is what that page looks like on the Google search results page:

New York Times Bestselling Author John Nance Returns To The Air ...
https://wildbluepress.com/**lockout**-john-j-**nance**-mystery-thriller/ ▾
★★★★★ Rating: 5 - 3 reviews
Nov 15, 2016 - Find out more about New York Times bestselling author John Nance's first #thriller novel with WildBlue Press, LOCKOUT with accolades from ...

2. All In One Schema.org Rich Snippets – this is a versatile free plugin that allows you to select the type of information on the page, then enter details about it into a form. It supports the following types of information: Reviews, events, people, products, recipes, software applications, videos, articles and services.

3. WP Rich Snippets – a paid plugin ($69 - $399/year)

with many add-ons that uses shortcodes also and provides rich snippet capabilities for WooCommerce reviews, data tables, software specs, locations and rich snippet boxes.

SOCIAL MEDIA SHARING PLUGINS

One way to maximize the online exposure of your content is to use a social media sharing plugin. When someone appreciates your content, then they can simply click an icon to share it in their favorite social network.

There are many social sharing plugins that you can find at http://wordpress.org/plugins/, and I have used many of them. I will recommend one because of its presentation and its analytics capability. The social sharing plugin I recommend is SumoMe. It places icons on the left-side of your pages like those on the left-side here.

SumoMe requires that you register with their site to use it, and once registered you'll have many other tools available. Most of them are premium that cost on a monthly basis. For example, they have tools like heatmaps that show you where people are (or are not) clicking on the site. Google analytics integration is free.

REDIRECT ALL OLD WEBSITE PAGES TO NEW PAGES – A CRITICAL TASK

One of the biggest mistakes made when creating a new website to replace an old one is that when the new site goes live, the old page URLs have been replaced with new ones and there is no redirect from the old page URLs to the new ones. That effectively removes all of the old pages on the site from the Internet and produces errors. All of the links pointing to the old pages are now broken links, and you have effectively killed most of the SEO that the old site had.

This problem can be avoided.

You need to start with obtaining a list of all of the pages from the old site. This usually means getting the sitemap file as a starting point. It is typically found at http://yourdomain.com/sitemap.xml or http://yourdomain.com/sitemap_index.xml. If you don't have a sitemap, then create one for free here:

https://www.xml-sitemaps.com/

I have used this tool for years. It allows you to create customized sitemaps and set them up to run automatically.

That will get you a complete list of the pages on your site. The next step is to grab all of the URLs and put them into a text file. You'll need to do a search and replace to remove the front part of the URL with your domain. You'll remove the bolded text in the two examples below, *but leave the slash / after the .com.*

http://yourdomain.com/**anarticleyouwrote.htm**

or

http://yourdomain.com/**an-article-you-wrote/**

Using the two examples above, the remaining text that you should use in your file would be:

/anarticleyouwrote.htm

or

/an-article-you-wrote/

Place the resulting URLs into the second column of an Excel spreadsheet. In the third column place the *full URL* of the page each should be redirected to. There should be one for each row of URLs you pasted in previously.

In the first column place this text in every row that had text in column two.:

redirect 301

This is what your spreadsheet should look like now:

redirect 301 /anarticleyouwrote.htm   http://yourdomain.com/an-improved-article/

Now copy all of the text and paste it into a text file. Do a search and replace to replace all tabs with a space. I have used NoteTab Pro for many years for this purpose. I search for ^T, replace it with a space then do a Replace All. The end result would look something like this:

redirect 301 /anarticleyouwrote.htm http://yourdomain. com/an-improved-article/

redirect 301 /an-old-article / http://yourdomain. com/a-better-article/

You now have the text that you can paste into the bottom of your .htaccess file in the root folder of your website. The .htaccess file is in the root folder of your website. Download it via FTP, *save a copy for backup,* then edit the file. Place a comment line like this just above where you pasted in the redirect code. It is always a good idea to add your initials like I did below:

```
# 7/17/2017 MAC Added 301 SEO Friendly
redirects
```

Underneath that comment, paste the text you edited and copied out of the text file. Save the file and upload it via FTP into the root folder of your website. Test the home page and a few other pages to see if they work. If not then upload your backup .htaccess file and go through the text file one line at a time to make sure every line is in the format of the two example lines above. Once you have made all corrections, re-upload the file and be ready with your backup again. Make sure to test a few pages before walking away from it.

SETUP ROBOTS.TXT FILES TO ALLOW CONTENT INDEXING

The robots.txt file is also in the root folder of your website. It tells the search engines what files and folders that you do not want them to index and put into their databases for everyone else to find. *This is not a guarantee that it won't happen,* but just an indicator to them that you don't want them to grab your content. Most of the major search engines abide by it.

The Wordpress files and folders recommended for you to block in your robots.txt file has changed through the years. Since Google actually renders the page content on your site now, when they go to a page that can't be rendered because it is being blocked by robots.txt then you get penalized. This includes javascript and css files and anything in your /wp-includes/ or /wp-admin/ folders.

According to Joost de Valk[25], the current best settings are to allow the search engines to index all of your content. This then is the recommended setting for your robots.txt file:

```
User-Agent: *
```

If you have private folders with content that you don't want to be found in the search engines then add a line like this:

```
Disallow: /yourprivatefolder/
```

Once you have determined the contents of your robots.txt file then you can make the changes in Yoast's SEO plugin settings in your Wordpress admin panel at SEO > Tools > File Editor. You can alternatively save the changes in a robots.txt text file then upload it to the root folder of your site via FTP.

CREATE AND INSTALL A FAVICON AND AN APPLE ICON

To best represent your company's branding, you always want to create a favicon and an Apple icon, so your website displays the best in all browsers. This is what it looks like when you use a favicon:

---

25   Wordpress robots.txt example for great SEO, Joost de Valk, https://yoast.com/wordpress-robots-txt-example/, (February 21, 2017)

The Apple icon appears on the screen of an iOS device like iPhones, iPads and iPods. To install these icons onto your site do the following:

1. Create two transparent png icons from your logo, one that is that is 32x32 pixels for the favicon, and one that is 57x57 pixels for the Apple Icon.

2. FTP up both icons to your themes images folder.

3. Add the following code to the header of your site. The place to add it within Wordpress is usually in the Theme Settings folder:

```
<link rel="apple-touch-icon" href="/
images/mycompany-apple-icon.png" />
<link rel="icon" href="https://
mydomain.com/wp-content/themes/child-
theme/images/favicon.png" />
```

4. Note that both methods of referencing the images above work – the relative reference that starts with / images/, and the full, explicit URL starting with http://.

> FOR FUTURE REFERENCE, DOWNLOAD A COPY OF THE ENTIRE OLD WEBSITE AND COPY IT INTO YOURDOMAIN.COM/OLD/

Before launching the new website, make a complete backup of the old one and put it into a folder named /old/. You'll need to FTP download all images, css and javascript files, plugins, databases, etc., save them on your local machine then upload them into the /old/ folder of the new site.

This allows you to refer to all pages and content of the old site in the future. You may be interested in the content of an old page, or the URL so you can do a redirect. Having a copy of the old site handy makes referencing the content a simple effort.

Here's how you do it:

1. Download WinHTTrack here for free and install it: http://www.httrack.com/

2. Download the entire old website to your local hard drive.

3. Upload the website into the /old/ folder of the new site so that the old home page opens up when you browse to http://yourdomain.com/old/.

4. Map out the old folder and files in http://yourdomain.com/robots.txt so the old files won't be indexed by the search engines. You just need to add a line like this:

```
Disallow: /old/
```

FINAL PRE-FLIGHT CHECKLIST

The content creator and editors, developer and site stakeholders should each do a final review of every site page and fix all problems before going live. Make sure the content is correct and all functionality works as designed. You don't want to announce to the world a website that has typos or incorrect information. Many times the website effort gets rushed and doesn't get the appropriate personnel's attention to the content before it goes live. What happens next is that customers (or potential customers) start sending emails to people in the company that they can't access certain areas like downloadable white papers, or that some of the content has errors or doesn't make sense. You don't want to deal with this.

Here are some of the checks you should complete before launching your site to ensure that it puts your company in the best light at launch time:

1. Verify that the home page content is clean and represents your company in the most positive light. That page gets most of the site traffic, so make

sure it presents your offers, products and services appropriately. Make sure it indicates your benefits to the visitor and isn't just a sales pitch.

2. Run your most important pages through the W3C HTML Markup validation service at https://validator.w3.org/ and correct any problems to make sure that you don't have HTML errors in the common areas of your content like the header, footer and sidebars that would be propagated through all site pages.

3. Verify your sites mobile-friendliness at https://search.google.com/search-console/mobile-friendly. Fix all issues that it discovers.

4. Run the site through WebCEO and Raven Reports to discover any site architecture, content or SEO issues and correct them all. Use the free services WebCEO and Raven Tools Site Auditor. They'll find problems that you could never discover on your own.

5. Verify that the footer content is a priority to the primary stakeholders. Standard and important footer content that you may want to be available on every footer of your site are

    a. Offers

    B. A listing of your main products or services

    C. How to download your mobile app

    d. Your copyright information similar to

Copyright © 20XX Your Company Name. All rights reserved.

    E. Sitemap link

    F. Privacy Policy link

    G. Contact us information and/or link

    H. Terms of use link

    I. Social media icons to connect with you at

all accounts

J. List of social media posts

K. Site search box

L. A different version of your logo. I usually place a black and white or gray version of the logo at the bottom-left.

M. Logos for awards you have received or a list of "As Seen On" logos where you or your members have been interviewed on TV or radio.

6. Verify that the content on your key pages and landing pages is appropriate since those pages are where you are sending your traffic via SEO, PPC and on-site calls to action.

7. Do page load time tests on your key pages at all of the sites listed in the "Website Performance Tools" section above and optimize each of those pages.

8. Verify that all of your most important pages have calls to action that send site visitors to your landing pages.

9. Subscribe to your email list through *every one of your landing pages* and verify that each form works and that your name and email is actually added to your email list. You'll have to use different emails, and you can even use fake ones when you run out of your own emails, but with your real email make sure you get all of the correspondence you should. Once the testing is complete, delete the fake ones from your email list.

10. Secure certificate - if you are going to move the final website to a different server and the old site uses a secure certificate, then you need to install a certificate on the new hosting server.

11. Before making the site live, test every form on the site

and make sure the emails go to all of the appropriate personnel. If this isn't done you'll stop receiving website leads. If they go to multiple people then you can create a cPanel forward address like sales@yourdomain.com and forward all emails that go to it to each of your personnel that should receive those emails.

TASKS REQUIRED TO LAUNCH WEBSITE

This is the final checklist to launch your new website and make it live. It ensures minimal risk to your website and your email accounts.

BACK UP/TRANSFER ALL FILES, RESTORE DATABASE

If you need to move your website to a different location (server) after you have built it, then you have to perform this step. If not then you can move to the next section.

FTP download all of the following files from your old server to the new hosting location:

1. The .htaccess and wp-config.php files in the root folder of your website
2. All files in the /wp-content/uploads folder
3. All files in the /wp-content/themes folder
4. All files in the /wp-content/plugins folder

Next, create a backup of the database as mentioned above.

Now FTP upload the files listed above to their respective locations on the new server and restore your backed up database into the database of your new Wordpress installation using phpMyAdmin. Make sure the config.php database settings point to the new database.

CHANGE ALL URLS IN DATABASE TO NEW URL

Before performing this operation make sure that you have backed up the database either using a plugin or with phpMyAdmin. You're going to make wholesale changes to the database, so a backup is important.

WORDPRESS WEBSITES FOR BUSINESS | 195

If your website was built using a temporary URL in a subfolder of your main website, or it was given to you by the hosting company then you need to change all temp URL database references to your proper domain name. The best way I have found to accomplish this in completely correct fashion is to use the special tool mentioned below.

MySQL data structures have two places where all data is stored. One is the value itself and the other is the *length* of the value. If you only change the value and not the length of that data item then you have effectively broken the database. This tool performs a search and replace across all of the contents of the entire MySQL database.

The free tool you can use to make changes to all instances of the old URL to the new one can be accomplished using this tool. You can get it at

https://interconnectit.com/products/
search-and-replace-for-wordpress-databases/

You download it to your local machine, unzip the files to a local folder then upload them to the root folder of your website server. I usually change the name of the folder to something like /sr/ once they are on the server. Then browse to the folder at http://yourdomain.com/sr/. That will open up the application.

Once you have it open, you enter your search phrase and the text you want to replace it. Here are some examples of search phrases you should use. Note as well what is *not* included in the search phrase like http:// or an ending slash for the URLs. Here are some example tempory URLs that you might be replacing in your database:

yourdomain.com/developmentfolder

~serverusername.com

You'll replace it with something like this:

yourdomain.com

You can do a test run before actually changing any data in the database, and I highly suggest you use this option to verify that you are changing the right info.

ENABLE WORDPRESS SITE INDEXING

Everything is now ready for prime time. All files are in place and the database has all of the correct URL references. You now need to allow the search engines to index your content and place it into their databases for others to see. You do this by logging into Wordpress and navigating to Settings > Reading then uncheck the "Discourage search engines from indexing this site" checkbox at the bottom and click the Save Changes button.

ENABLE SITE INDEXING VIA THE ROBOTS.TXT FILE

As mentioned above, log into Wordpress and navigate to SEO > Tools > File Editor and edit your robots.txt file. Place this into it then save your changes:

```
# allow everything to be indexed
# per https://yoast.com/wordpress-
robots-txt-example/
#   and http://www.robotstxt.org/
robotstxt.html
User-agent: *
Disallow: /old/
```

This code basically allows search engines to index all of the content on your site except for the /old/ folder content. The first three lines are comments, and I recommend that you place them into the file for your own reference in case you want to learn more about why we are using these settings.

MANAGE DNS RECORDS (TECHNICAL) – CONNECTING TO THE INTERNET

Every computer on the Internet has a physical address called an Internet Protocol (IP) address that represents the physical location at which it can be directly accessed. A typical IP address would be 123.45.67.890. That is an older version of IP address called IPv4. IPv4 addresses have a limitation of 2^{32} addresses, or just over 4 billion addresses. That has nine zeros. Because of the explosion of the Internet, and the *Internet of things*, there is a much bigger need for IP addresses. Basically we'll run out of addresses using IPv4 in the near future.

Because of this, a newer version of IP addressing is now in use called IPv6. IPv6 allows 2^{128} addresses, or roughly 3.4 x 10^{38}. That's 38 zeros after the 3.4, and it should do well for us far into the future. A typical IPv6 address would be 3ffe:1900:4545:3:200:f8ff:fe21:67cf which is a series of eight hexadecimal (0 – 9 then a – f to represent a total of 16) characters separated by colons.

We know websites by human readable names called domain names. They are managed on the Internet by Domain Name Servers (DNS). DNS server software translates a domain name into an IP address and handles requests sent to that domain. A DNS server routes Internet traffic to the appropriate web server computer by grabbing its internally stored DNS records then routing the request appropriately.

Your website addressing and management of the email tied to your domain (person@yourdomain.com) are closely tied together and both are managed by DNS records. When you set up or move your hosting you need to be aware of whether you want both your website and email to be managed at your hosting company or not. If you want them both managed by your hosting company then you typically change the nameservers at your registrar like GoDaddy or Network Solutions. Nameservers are the values retrieved by the DNS server when your domain is addressed. If you want your website to be at one hosting company and your email managed somewhere else, then you need to make MX (Mail Exchange) or A-record changes to your DNS records. All of this is explained below.

An important item to note before you make any of the changes discussed below: I highly recommend that you consult with tech support at both your registrar and your website and email hosting companies before making any changes yourself. They'll be happy to guide you down the road to make the correct changes, and may even do it for you, so don't make any changes that you don't feel comfortable making yourself. You have them as a safety net so you *must* take advantage of it.

MONITOR THE DNS CHANGES YOU MAKE BELOW

Below you'll read about making changes and the delays incurred for the changes to propagate across the entire Internet. You can monitor the speed of those changes by going to this site:

https://www.whatsmydns.net/#NS/

Just type in your domain name and you'll see the actual values of the nameserver, MX, or A-record changes as they progress through the main DNS servers across the Internet.

You'll see a list of servers from all over the world (20 at the time of this writing), and when you successfully make changes to your DNS settings you'll be able to see the new values propagate in real-time across the Internet.

IF YOU WANT TO MOVE BOTH YOUR WEBSITE AND YOUR EMAIL MANAGEMENT

When you want to move both your website as well as management of your emails from one hosting company to another, you need to change the nameservers at your registrar. Your registrar is where you bought your domain name. You can also purchase your domain name at your hosting company, or any one of hundreds of other registrar companies, and if so then that is where you'll have to go to change your nameservers.

To make your website and email live on a new hosting company's server you need to point your nameservers to the new hosting company. They'll give you the right values, and there should be two of them, a primary and a secondary nameserver. They'll be something like this: ns1.hostingcompany.com and ns2.hostingcompany.com. I won't explain how to make the changes because it is done differently at every registrar, so you'll have to ask your registrar how to make the changes or have them do it.

Before you change your nameservers you should have all of the emails and forwards set up at the new hosting company. A forward just redirects an email sent to one address to a different one. If your emails and forwards aren't set up at the new hosting before you change the nameservers then everyone's email will be dead after you change the nameservers and move to the new hosting. More on this in the "Tool To Simplify Moving Your Emails To A New Server" section below.

Nameserver Propagation Delay

After you make your nameserver changes and save them it will take twenty-four to forty-eight hours for those changes to propagate across the entire Internet so that they are installed on all Internet DNS servers. It takes this long for all of the DNS servers on the Internet to obtain the new value and route requests for your domain to the right place. You might see your website come up on your local machine within half an hour to an hour, but the rest of the Internet won't see it consistently until your new nameserver values have propagated into the DNS servers of the entire Internet.

IF YOU JUST WANT TO MOVE YOUR WEBSITE, NOT YOUR EMAIL MANAGEMENT

In this case you change only the IP address of the A-record named @ to point to your new hosting. You'll change the value of the @ record to the IP address of your new server. Your hosting company will provide you with the IP address.

After making the A-record change you can expect a four to eight hour propagation delay before the changes take affect across the entire Internet.

IF YOU JUST WANT TO MOVE YOUR EMAIL MANAGEMENT, NOT YOUR WEBSITE

If you only want to move your email hosting and management, then you have a couple options. You can change the IP address of the A-records on your existing server to point to the new location where you want to manage your email, or you can point the mail exchange (MX) records at your new hosting company to point to the new location, then change your nameservers. The latter case is for the scenario where your new hosting will not be managing your email.

How do you determine where to make these MX or A-record changes you ask? I'm glad you asked that question. That is determined by the nameserver values (pointers) at your registrar. The hosting company that the nameservers point to is where your DNS records are managed, so that is where you need to make the MX or A-record changes. The values you use will be given to you by your email provider.

After making MX or A-record changes you can expect a four to eight hour propagation delay before the changes kick in across the entire Internet.

INTERNET OF THINGS

By the way, *the Internet of things* refers to the network of devices (things) that contain an IP address and are connected to the Internet. Things can be house alarms, automobile tire pressure gauges, temperature sensors, vehicle GPS devices, human heart monitors, RFID chips injected into animals for identification, refrigerator product detection devices and just about anything you can think of that someone would like to monitor or communicate with. This is why we need a lot of IP addresses.

MOVE EXISTING EMAILS FROM ONE SERVER TO ANOTHER USING IMAP

Before starting this process, read the next section for an automated solution.

If you store your emails on your server and not your local machine, then you have to move those emails to the new hosting server. This will have to be done for every email account you have in your domain that stores email on the server and not locally. It is a tricky process that can be simplified with the right tools.

To move your emails to a new server you need to create IMAP email accounts on both your old and new servers. That will maintain a constant connection that allows you to move the emails from one account to another. There are basically two type of email accounts, IMAP (Internet Messaging Access Protocol) and POP3 (Post Office Protocol). Each is a protocol of communication between your email client software and the online mail server. You generally use a POP3 account when you only manage your emails from one device or a desktop computer and download them to your local computer. You use IMAP when you manage your email with multiple devices and want to leave the emails on the server and not your device. We'll use an IMAP protocol account to move your emails from the old to the new server without losing any of them.

Moving your emails from one server to another can take one to three days because of the propagation delays mentioned above. You move the emails from the live server to the temporary, development server in one effort. Then you make your nameserver, MX or A-record changes, wait till the propagation is over then move the remaining emails again to the new server.

To accomplish this you'll need the IMAP settings and login info from both servers which will include:

1. Username and password
2. Port number
3. Server IP address. Don't use the domain name. Your hosting companies can provide this information to you.

Create an IMAP account in your email client (like Microsoft Outlook or Mozilla Thunderbird for Windows, or Apple Mail) that points to the same email account (like yourname@yourdomain.com) on both of the servers. The account that you have been using will show all of your emails and folders, and the other will be blank with no emails or folders. If this is a new IMAP account on the server that you have been using for months, then make sure all of your emails appear in the account before copying them to the new server. It can take hours to download all of your emails if you have been saving them for months on the old server.

Next you'll copy your emails from the old to the new server accounts *within your email client*. Once both accounts are created, connected, and all emails have been synced to the old server, then you can drag and drop the folders and emails from the old account to the new. Do it on a folder by folder basis, so you don't lock up your email client software.

After you make the nameserver/MX/A-record changes to make the new mail server live at the new location you have to go through this process again to move the files that have come in during the propagation.

The tool mentioned below makes this process fairly painless, and I highly recommend that you use it to move your emails from one server to another.

> *Tool To Simplify Moving Your Emails To A New Server*

Alternatively you can use a third-party service like the one at https://transfermyemail.ca/shop/. It costs $1.99/day, so it won't break the bank, and it's a small cost to get your emails transferred safely. You just need the IMAP settings and login info mentioned above to connect to both servers to move your emails. It is a simple process and an extremely useful service.

AFTER-LAUNCH TASKS

CREATE THEN REGISTER A GEOSITEMAP WITH GOOGLE

If you are a local company, then one of the sitemaps you need to create is a geositemap. This file defines the physical location of your company. It contains the latitude and longitude of your address and is used by Google to place your company in Google Maps.

There is a great tool at http://geositemapgenerator.com/ that you can use to create your geositemap. Type your company's information including your address into it to create the files you need. Then download the two files geositemap.xml and locations.kml to your local hard drive. Next FTP the files to the root folder of your web server which makes them available to be read by the search engines.

This tool has a multi-location capability by uploading a CSV text file with all of the name, address, phone number and description info for each of your company locations.

This file is important since it is used by Google to place your company at its physical location. For local companies Google then looks for you in the most important local citation directories and compares the information in those directories with that of your geositemap.xml file. They lastly check for reviews of your company in those same directories. If you have all of this in place then you will be blessed with top local rankings in Google, Bing and Yahoo! – assuming you take the step I describe next.

REGISTER YOUR SITEMAPS AT GOOGLE SEARCH CONSOLE AND BING WEBMASTER TOOLS

To make sure that the search engines index all of your site's content – and the content you add to it in the future, you need to register your sitemaps at Google Search Console (formerly Google Webmaster Tools) and Bing Webmaster Tools. Yahoo registration is now managed at Bing. Create accounts at both places then proceed with the instructions below.

Once you have created the account at Google Search Console and Bing Webmaster Tools, you need to verify that you own the site. There are multiple methods to do this. The one I prefer is to download a file from each of the sites, then upload the same file into the root folder of your website. Once you have done this you need to click the Verify button then Google and Bing will know that you own the website, and you'll be able to proceed with registering your sitemap files.

The sitemap that is created by the Yoast SEO plugin is located at:

http://yourdomain.com/sitemap_index.xml

and your geo sitemap is at:

http://yourdomain.com/geositemap.xml

In Google Search Console click the Dashboard screen and you'll see the Sitemaps link. Click it, submit your sitemap URLs and test each one. If they pass then submit each to Google.

In Google Search Console you also need to set the preferred URL for your site. Do this by clicking the gear icon at the top-right then selecting Site Settings. Note that this setting should be the same as what you have in Wordpress > Settings > General > Wordpress Address (URL) and Site Address (URL). You can change this setting in Google Search Console when you select your site then click the gear icon at the top-right and select Site Settings. Select either the URL with or without the www (same as Wordpress settings), then save your changes.

In Bing Webmaster Tools go to Dashboard > Configure My Site > Sitemaps > Submit A Sitemap, and submit your sitemaps from the URLs above.

This is the first step in ensuring that you are on the radar of both search engines, and that they see your new content as you add it.

FINAL CHECKOUT

Ok, so you've built the site, you love your content and it looks great. You've covered all of your services and have landing pages and calls to action pointing to each of them. Are you good to go and ready to launch it? Probably not.

There are so many components and sections of the site that can cause problems for you. Many are very difficult to find without good tools. Here are some of the problems that these tools can reveal to avoid problems that can drag your sites performance down and fly under your radar:

- A few images on key pages have huge file sizes.
- You have used the same title or meta-description on multiple pages.
- You have other duplicate content issues.
- You have performance issues on your most important pages.
- You haven't enabled indexing in Wordpress.
- Your robots.txt file blocks the indexing of your site or important pages on it.
- You have broken links.
- You have missing images that drag down your page load times.
- You have too many plugins that slow down your page load times.
- Your site has other configuration problems that would otherwise be difficult to find.

Using the tools below will do an overall performance check, so you can be confident that when you launch your site that it's success will not be hindered by hidden problems like this.

GATHER BROKEN LINKS FROM GOOGLE SEARCH CONSOLE, CORRECT WITH AN .HTACCESS 301 REDIRECT

You can lose a lot of SEO value if there are broken links pointing to non-existent pages of your site. This can happen in any of the following cases:

- If you have changed from one website to another
- If you constantly add *and modify* content and page URLs. Updating content is generally a good thing, but when you add links to your site then change the URL it introduces a broken link unless you fix it by pointing to the new URL in all places.
- You have links to pages that have been replaced by other pages with a different URL.

The following will correct all of the problems listed above. What you need to do is log into Google Search Console and navigate to Crawl > Crawl Errors > Not Found. There will be a list of broken links that you should fix. You can do this by adding a line for each of the broken links to the .htaccess file in your websites root folder. The line would look like this:

```
redirect 301 /brokenlinkpage/ http://
yourdomain.com/redirect-page/
```

The 301 means that it is a permanent redirect, and passes the most SEO juice from the broken link to another relevant page. Create a redirect like this in your .htaccess file for each of the links in the Crawl Errors. This was explained in more detail earlier in this book.

USE ONLINE TOOLS TO SCAN FOR SERIOUS ERRORS BEFORE LIFTOFF

Here are a few tools that you can use to scan your site. I recommend starting from the top and going down. If you spend the recommend amount of time on each of them then you should have a good idea of the health of your site. The times recommended below are just for set up and analysis, not the time it takes to fix the problems that you find.

Web Page Test – Most Important Pages, Home Page Minimum – 1 Hour

http://webpagetest.org

Enter the URLs of your most important pages and look for red lines across the chart from left to right. Those are missing objects. Also look for other objects that are taking too long to load, then fix them all.

Screaming Frog – 1 – 2 Hours of Analysis

https://www.screamingfrog.co.uk/seo-spider/#download

This is a desktop tool that has to be installed on your local computer. Do so then use it to test for many SEO factors. Here is a guide on how to get the most out of it:

http://www.seoblog.com/2016/03/guide-screaming-frog/

Web CEO – Start with the Free Version – 1 Hour to Set up, Analyze

http://webceo.com

Sign up with the free option, then when you're logged in go to Reports > Consolidated Reports. Go into the report settings by clicking the gear icon, then click report contents to check each of the data items you want to see in your report. You can also send automatic reports to yourself via email.

You can then download the report. Do this, then correct all of the most egregious problems identified by the WebCEO report.

Raven Tools - $99/mo. – 1 Hour to Set up and Analyze Reports

http://raventools.com

Raven Tools saved one of our campaigns at Well.org (I'm an owner and past CTO of Well.org). We were bringing PPC traffic to a landing page that wasn't converting in the least. I ran a Raven Tools report on the site, and we found that one of the images was 42mb in size, and it made the page take forever to load. We fixed the image and started getting conversions. Another problem that this report discovered was that after launch one of our sites robots.txt file was stopping search engines from indexing any of the content on the site. Correcting this quickly resulted in the site being found in Google.

After signing up, run their Site Auditor report to find hidden problems with your site.

Deep Crawl - $49/mo. – 1 Hour to Set up and Analyze Reports

http://deepcrawl.com

Another tool that will analyze your entire site. Their reports aren't as friendly as Raven Tools, but it is another data point to make sure your site is healthy before launching.

SET UP A CONTENT DELIVERY NETWORK (CDN)

The reason I added the CDN topic at the end of this book is because a CDN adds a layer of caching that has to be cleared every time you change content and want to view it on your website. This becomes a nuisance if you are in the middle of development. Once you have finalized the development and content of your website, and it has stabilized after having been running for a few to several weeks, then it is time to add a CDN. This also fits in with the server optimization information I wrote about above, but I'm adding it here to avoid the issues you will run into if you add a CDN prematurely.

The normal scenario of delivering your websites content without a CDN is that your content is delivered from your hosting company's server. A single server. This means that anyone in the world requesting your content will have it delivered from that one server computer. It's not ideal, and that is where a CDN comes in.

A content delivery network, commonly referred to as a CDN, is a distributed network of proxy servers that serve your websites content from computers close in proximity to the computer that requests the information. Proxy meaning that these computers serve your websites content in place of your actual website server when your company's content is requested.

The benefits of a CDN are that your website will load much faster than without it. You can expect much faster page loading at fractions of your load times without it.

Setting up a CDN is a very technical effort and should always be done with your website hosting company involved. If you don't have the proper technical expertise on your team I guarantee you will have problems.

An important topic to be aware of is that, if your email is hosted at a different location than your website, then the MX record IP address will be different than your website's hosting IP address. It is advisable to ask your hosting company *and* CDN company what all of the DNS records will be before the nameserver change to your CDN. Once you have this list then present it to your website hosting and email hosting companies and have them verify that the settings are correct, *and that your email will continue to operate after the switch to your CDN is complete!* If not then you'll lose connection to your emails during this propagation, so this is a critical consideration.

Considering the above, the actual settings and final effort involved to add a CDN to your website are fairly simple. You swap the nameservers at your registrar from those of your hosting company to those of your CDN. Your CDN and your current hosting company will give you the values you need.

After you make the nameserver change to your new CDN you'll have to wait twenty-four to forty-eight hours for the changes to take full effect across the Internet due to DNS propagation times, so any inconsistencies that you see before this propagation is complete should settle out when it is over. Have patience.

Most of the top hosting companies have direct relationships with CDN companies like Cloudflare. Ask your hosting company if this is the case, and if so then use their processes to install their recommended CDN. Many times cPanel has it integrated directly into their interface.

CREATE SITE DOCUMENTATION

After your website is up and running as described above, I recommend that you create a Word document that contains all of the following information and logins so you'll only have one place to go when you need to manage any part of the site. One of the most annoying problems I see people and companies dealing with is that they can't find the login to their site, control panel or social media accounts. Creating this documentation will solve this problem. This is what you want in it:

1. Registrar (where you bought your domain), cPanel and Wordpress logins

2. Nameserver settings

3. Website IP address

4. FTP Login

5. Instructions on how to manage the standard and customized sections of your site like how to add sliders, how to manage featured products and where the theme documentation is.

6. Email server info

7. Wordpress database name, server and login info

8. Social media logins

I have provided you with sample documentation in the resources section below.

BOOK RESOURCES

All of the resources mentioned in this book, and those mentioned at the beginning of the book in the "Five Powerful Checklists, Online Tools" section can be acquired on this page:

http://wbp.bz/wordpresswebsitesresources

CONTACT ME – REALLY!

If you get stuck in any of this stuff, or you just have questions and you'd like to get some real answers then feel free to contact me via email at michael@wildbluepress.com. I'll be happy to answer your questions and get you through the issues you're facing. Obviously I can't spend hours coding your custom solutions, but I can get you headed in the right direction, so go ahead and reach out.

ACKNOWLEDGEMENTS

I have been fortunate in this life to be exposed to books in many ways and from different directions. This has put ideas into my head for years. Ideas that told me I should be telling my own story. I have always been a reader, but when my wife Lauri Ver Schure became the owner of Murder by the Book, a mystery bookstore in Denver, Colorado, I was exposed to the business of book selling. So many interesting authors came through for book signings to tell their stories, and some of them came around several times, so I was fortunate to become friends with so many great authors and to have such a wonderful wife whose favorite pastime is to curl up on the couch with her latest favorite book.

My friend and partner at WildBlue Press, New York Times bestselling author Steve Jackson, has provided so much conversation and insight into the inner workings of being an author and of the publishing world that we were both motivated to create a publishing company that does it all better, a publishing company for the benefit of authors. WildBlue Press is the brainchild of those thoughts and conversations. Steve continues to lend his experience towards this exciting venture. Forty authors and sixty books later, we're growing and learning every day.

To get WildBlue Press started there were three accomplished writers that took the plunge and signed up to be our first authors – Burl Barer, Ron Franscell and Caitlin Rother deserve special thanks. Their vote of confidence in Steve and me, and this WildBlue Press venture is the highest compliment you can give someone. Since then we have signed many authors and published a slew of great books. All of this activity of getting outstanding stories into the hands of our great fans is truly motivating. It is impossible to engage in the processes of publishing books without having some of it rub off, and all of the authors we work with have served as inspiration indeed. Special thanks to all of our authors at WildBlue Press.

Every day at WildBlue Press is challenging. Things break and our team fixes them. We are so fortunate to have a group of dedicated individuals making sure that each book we publish is of the highest quality in many ways, and that our content and website are in order. Thanks to the team at WildBlue Press – Production Manager Ashley Butler, Special Projects Manager Amanda Luedeke, Finance Director Lauri Ver Schure, Art Director Carla Jackson, Cover Designer/ Formatter Elijah Toten, Editor Andrea Ferak, Editor Mary Kay Wayman, Editor Jacqueline Gallman, Cover Designer Kim Mesman, and our Social Media Manager Adam Buongiovanni. Their tireless work in producing high-quality books, eBooks and audio books have inspired me to write this book.

On the subject of building websites, I have so many clients to thank for paying me to express my ideas and grow their businesses by building websites and doing the online marketing and advertising for their companies. A couple are noteworthy because I have consulted with them for years integrating the latest and best tools and technologies to solve their most difficult problems and increase sales for their companies – David Sauers of Royal Restrooms and Todd Reade of Transmagic. Without the employment of these clients, and others like them to design and build their websites and carry out their online marketing and advertising I would not have had the knowledge to write this book.

I also want to thank my friend and the best outright designer I have every worked with, Phil Dineen of Designo.com. We've worked out many tough problems in the wee hours of the morning.

OTHER WILDBLUE PRESS BOOKS BY MICHAEL CORDOVA

PRODUCTIVITY TOOLS FOR BUSINESS
57 Proven Online Tools to Recapture the Hours of Your Day

Productivity Tools for Business details
http://wbp.bz/57tools

INFORMATION ABOUT MICHAEL CORDOVA
https://wildbluepress.com/authors/michael-cordova-bio/
http://www.21stsoft.com/about-us/
http://linkedin.com/in/michaelcordova

222 | MICHAEL CORDOVA

REVIEW THE BOOK

Word-of-mouth is critical to an author's long-term success. If you appreciated this book please leave a review on the Amazon sales page:

http://wbp.bz/ww4ba

For More News About Michael Cordova Signup For Our Newsletter:

http://wbp.bz/newsletter

224 | MICHAEL CORDOVA

CALL FOR BUSINESS BOOKS

Do you have an idea for a business book? Have you honed your services to perfection and would like to get a book into the hands of many more people than you can help directly? A book that you have authored is also the ticket to speaking engagements that will expand your reach even further. If you'd like to discuss the possibilities then visit our Interested Authors page at WildBlue Press and let us know what you're thinking. We're happy to discuss book publishing options with you.

226 | MICHAEL CORDOVA

DISCLOSURE/DISCLAIMER

I have carefully combed through the tools that I have used for many years in my business within this book, and I have an affiliate relationship with the providers of some of the products or services I have mentioned. As such, I may be compensated monetarily when you purchase from those providers. You should always perform due diligence before buying goods or services from anyone via the Internet or offline. I am disclosing this in accordance with the Federal Trade Commission's 16 CFR, Part 255: "Guides Concerning the Use of Endorsements and Testimonials in Advertising."

To the maximum extent permitted by applicable law, the author and publisher exclude all representations, warranties, undertakings and guarantees relating to this book. Without prejudice to the generality of the foregoing paragraph, the author and publisher do not represent, warrant, undertake or guarantee that the information in the book is correct, accurate, complete or non-misleading, and that the use of the guidance in this book will lead to any particular outcome or result.

Although the author and publisher have made every effort to ensure that the information in this book was correct at press time, the author and publisher do not assume and hereby disclaim any liability to any party for any loss, damage, or disruption caused by errors or omissions, whether such errors or omissions result from negligence, accident, or any other cause.

The products and services mentioned in this book are truly recommended by me based on my personal experience with them, and my opinion is that they are the best on the market for the purposes described.

228 | MICHAEL CORDOVA

ANOTHER BUSINESS BOOK FROM WILDBLUE PRESS

CORPORATE SUPERPOWER
Cultivating A Winning Culture For Your Business

Corporate Superpower details
http://wbp.bz/CSpower

SAMPLE CHAPTER NEXT

CHAPTER ONE

LIVE, IMMATERIAL, AND FUNCTIONAL

Since the time of Cicero, people have tended to take the phenomenon of culture for granted, often assuming that it is synonymous with organizational culture. However, a more specialized understanding of organizational culture began to coalesce some decades ago. In fact, it was first described as a group climate by Lewin, Lippitt, and White in 1939. Subsequently, in the mid-seventies, organizational norms, roles, and values were viewed in terms of the social psychology of organizations, although, at that stage, it was not explicitly stated as organizational climate or culture. Since then, a large number of definitions have appeared, serving to confirm the complex nature of this incorporeal being. However, we are still exploring this elephant in a dark room.

Culture does not exist in an isolated and purified environment without the presence of other people. Culture is a complex phenomenon, deeply interpenetrating all of our daily activities, which exists only in collectives of people, i.e. in states, nations, and organizations. Culture is a system itself. The word "system" derives from the ancient Greek word systema which comes from two words – syn, which means "together", and histemi, which means "to set." System is actually an idea which defines how process or ideology is to be set for the best possible performance or outcome. Cultural or ideological systems can be seen as a collection of roles which reflect human values and thus have a direct impact on organizational results. As a system, culture needs to be viewed using a systematic approach and not a mono-dimensional view.

THREE DIMENSIONS OF CULTURE

Culture is multidimensional. One dimension is pragmatic and rational, regulating rules, norms, and codes of working in organizations. A second dimension is more irrational and incorporates the behavioral and psychological approach of the group's members to their duties and to the organization itself. A third dimension reflects the transcendent side of culture, which can be viewed as the organizational cathedral, the reference point for the entire organization's activity.

Regarding the strictly rational aspect, Aristotle wisely defined a state, as an interaction for reaching mutual goals. Not short-term tasks, but goals of successful survival, prosperity, mutual support, defense, and satisfaction of its own needs. Applying Aristotle's definition to an organizational viewpoint, we can say that it is similar to the purpose of the state, just on a smaller scale – an organization is the interaction of its members ordered to reach defined goals that benefit the organization.

Organisational Anatomy (Konovalov 2016, 71) defines organizational culture as a catalyzer of performance. I will use this definition in the present discussion as being the most advanced and practically relevant to the aims of all organizations. Looking at the spiritual or transcendent side, we can consider company culture as the soul of the organizational body, which helps the brain (management) motivate the body for action, sense the environment, attract stakeholders' positive emotions and energy, stimulate and encourage development, and drive the organization through tough times.

This third dimension is the dynamic power and spiritual core of the organization. It is built on symbols which shape the company's psychological state and define the boundaries of its influence. We will discuss the role of symbols and values in more detail later as this is a tremendously critical and under-appreciated issue.

Each of these facets of organizational culture empowers and enlightens the other sides of the immaterial core of any company, and by doing so, gives life and vitality to a company. Culture also defines the boundaries of an organization. Within those boundaries, dependent upon the culture's nature, the talents of the employees are revealed and allowed to flourish.

INDISPENSABLE CATALYZER

Production or providing of services can be compared with a complicated chemical reaction of long-chain utilization of resources by perfectly synergized functions. A chemical reaction is a change of two components – substance and energy. Substance, in this sense, represents all tangible and intangible resources and capabilities within an organization. Organizational culture is that energy which comes from the joint efforts and enthusiastic fulfillment of duties of all employees, and, as a result, adds spark and life to all processes. If the culture is positive and stimulating, then we can expect the desired reaction which results in a superior product and secures growth.

At the same time, we do not want culture to be a counterproductive energy, i.e. an inhibitor, which slows down substance transformation, making resource utilization costly and restricting the organization's growth. In a more rigorous way, there is a fit between strategy and culture which has a direct impact on company performance.

In a positive cultural environment, we become more productive and positively attuned toward colleagues. We speak with enthusiasm to friends about what we do, how important it is, and how good it is to work for our company. If the organization's members are effectively collaborating, positively and naturally attuned toward achieving company goals, this positive energy will aid in creating excellent products even if the materials used are less than perfect. Using culture to generate this level of enthusiasm and commitment is important for any company, established or start-up. Strong culture allows enhanced exploitation of people's competencies, reaching higher behavioral consistency among employees, and overall preparedness for necessary change.

IMMORTAL SOUL

A strong soul defines a healthy psychological state and provides strength. If one is going through challenges at a stage when muscles are prepared to give up, the soul pushes forward and thus achieves success. Also, it is important to understand that a company and its culture cannot be separated just as a human being and a soul cannot function independently of each other.

A group of people, even when working toward the same goal, remains a crowd without this intangible, yet vital, element of culture. Culture serves as a force which forms productive and collaborative teams. Culture is born as soon as founders start actively interacting in the creation of a business plan and establishing a new venture, even before the organization is fully formed. They are imprinting the first characteristics of culture, its nature and shape. Unfortunately, the issue of culture is usually a neglected conversation by entrepreneurs and start-up enthusiasts, often at the cost of a slow and ineffective start-up. Entrepreneurs and investors need to look into the cultural properties of a new project as a matter of priority, for in so doing, they will define future growth prospects which can predict future performance.

SPIRITUAL CORE

The spiritual core defined by culture is responsible for a sense of belonging, loyalty, pride, and a number of other crucial factors of productive organizational citizenship. Residing in symbols and a proclaimed understanding of the need for effective interaction towards organizational goals, cultural identity in any organization is as unique as human fingerprints and cannot be replicated anywhere else.

When we talk about a person we admire, a common characteristic we note is that this person is able to pull him or herself together when facing difficulties. A person who exhibits such spiritual strength is able to deliver extraordinary performance and reveal inner creativity in the face of adversity.

The same applies in businesses where spiritual identity permeates all operations and processes, forming a solid dome above a company, allowing it to withstand any problem. However, if a company's spiritual identity is weak, it is like being under a leaky shelter, eventually driving its people away.

A RATIONALITY OF IMMATERIAL BEING

A tree with roots that grow deep can withstand strong winds. The stronger and deeper the roots, the stronger the tree is. We cannot see these roots, but we can see the tree. If the roots are weak then the tree will have more of a withered appearance with a lot of dead branches. Likewise, organizational culture becomes strong only if it's built on action and interaction, i.e. active and effective collaboration and mutual support, and not just talking about possible success.

Managers tend to neglect to form an understanding of organizational culture and the vital role it plays in making the organization successful. Most often, managers receive training about leadership styles, ways to motivate staff, and corporate loyalty. Rarely does this involve discussions of the foundational role culture plays in a company. As a result, businesses face constant loss of seemingly loyal customers, valuable employees, and enthusiastic investors. We are consciously digging a pothole for the companies by turning toward seemingly rational opportunistic transactions. However, pure rationality is not enough in the management of such sensitive issues as loyalty, staff motivation, and customer satisfaction. In terms of internal environment, culture bridges a gap between purely functional working relationships and interpersonal relationships which are a substratum for nurturing tacit knowledge, reciprocity, and willingness to understand others.

Rationally bound actions often result in quick gains but often become less successful in the long term. The metaphysical role of culture in this phenomenon is underestimated. Without culture, all these aspirations and seemingly feasible plans become unrealistic.

Organizational culture has a tremendous number of roles due to its trifold nature. Culture is everywhere and in everything, from how people support colleagues, care for customers, solve problems, respect company achievements, and even to how a cup of coffee is offered to a visitor. We can feel a company's culture right from our first interaction with it. Culture gives a human appearance to the living body of an organization, thus making it attractive in the eyes of employees and customers. Its uniqueness can be seen in the organization's determination, persistence in achieving goals, desire for development, and spirit of creativity and innovation.

As Japanese writer Ryunosuke Satoro concisely stated, "Individually, we are one drop. Together, we are an ocean." By strengthening bonds between co-workers, culture makes them an ocean with a tremendously irresistible power to achieve phenomenal goals. If employees feel respected and appreciated, they no longer feel like separated drops but important parts of a greater whole, and as a result, they feel obliged to be productive, loyal, and engaged in company life. These critical attributes are seeded and nurtured by culture. Also, culture provides an adaptation mechanism which shapes and adjusts the mindsets of new recruits and revitalizes company veterans in line with organizational goals, thus securing stable long-term development.

Organizational processes and relations cannot be harmonic without a prominent positive culture. People-centered culture encourages an environment of collaboration, stimulating development of seamless and harmonic organizational processes. It is the key to balancing collective and individualistic behaviors and uniting them for one purpose.

Trust is the glue and stimulator of all relations, and no authentic business transaction can be executed without it. Trust is a macro-phenomenon which lubricates all internal and external processes. It strengthens relationships inside and outside the organization, helping to develop mutual support. A strong culture stimulates trust across the entire organization, building it from within and from without. By contrast, a weak culture is characterized by a breakdown of trust that will see the organization dissolve into isolated cliques with little to no communication between them.

Culture, and its transformations over a company's history, reflects the experiences of surviving in a challenging organizational environment. It reflects how organizational members have gone through extreme moments, withstood external forces, collaborated, and learned from each other. Thus, culture derives from a combination of the reflection of bad experiences, best practices, and advantages of mutual support.

For instance, a co-founder of a British transport company suggested that:

"We took care to nurture a supportive environment from day one that eventually allowed us to survive, learn from losses, value the role of each team member, learn how to work through socializing and become stronger as one body. Expensive trucks are nothing without effective people."

It is impossible to develop such human and social capitals without culture, which is critical for organizational existence. Human capital represents skills, talents, knowledge, experience, creativity, and know-how, which can flourish only in an environment of positive culture. By stimulating mutual support and development of productive internal and external organizational relations, culture is a great constructor of social capital which allows attracting resources embedded in external networks of relations. Culture makes an organization a social being and a responsible part of a society, which aids in attracting additional external support and the recognition of its contributions.

FUNCTIONS OF CULTURE

A modern American skeptic and writer, Phil Plait, in his talk The Goal of Skepticism, noted, "Give a man a truth and he will think for a day. Teach a man to reason and he will think for a lifetime." (Plait 2010) By understanding the reasons behind the very nature of organizational culture and its functions, we obtain food to fuel our thoughts and actions for a lifetime.

Let's imagine the product of a given business as a gold bar valued according to purity. It could be a product unit for producers, money or knowledge for knowledge-dependent organizations, the number of served customers for location-dependent organizations, saved lives for charities, or tax-paying citizens in a state. An equation to express the relationship between the gold and the activity which generates it would work by multiplying product units by hours worked, in which the product unit is something physical offered to customers. However, we also can add effort, motivation, or commitment into this equation as elements from another immeasurable and undefined dimension – the strength of organizational culture. The equation will then read: product unit x hours x cultural strength which will result in a gold bar of 24-karat value. However, should the culture be counterproductive, i.e. have negative value; the value of the final product will be significantly reduced.

It is common to think that a product only comes out of a workshop as the result of physical resources and energy. Such an outlook overlooks the psychological components of the organization. Understandably, it is easy to concentrate on what we can see, and touch; tangible items that we can fix. However, the real strength of any organization comes not from its physical resources but from more intangible, more qualitative elements.

We can define culture as organizational metaphysics. This is the physics of managing human emotions and senses. The difference between successful and unsuccessful business lies in understanding this.

The inner psychological state of the organization is reflected in the functions of culture. The functions are: the inner organization's language, praxis or active doing, apoptosis or controlled cells death, homeostasis or cultural system regulator, and entropy or energy regulator. We will discuss these critical functions in greater details further in this chapter.

LANGUAGE

Culture differs based on context. Whether we walk into a university, church, fishmonger shop, or a Navy ship, there will be differences in culture, an often-overlooked reality. The clearest difference is that each organization has its own unique language. By recalling Terry Pratchett's The Colour of Magic (2008), we may say that the organizational universe is full of different discs with their own cultures and thus their own standards and languages. From this viewpoint, language reflects a nature, structure, and description of roles in a cultural domain.

Language defines the art of transmitting and reading signals between people. Language defines communication as a vehicle of transmitting messages and stories between people without losing the quality of human emotions and perspectives. It defines the use of acceptable and forbidden metaphors. Language describes values and allows them to be communicated to all corners of the cultural territory.

Consider legendary hero Jason and his Argonauts in their chase for the Golden Fleece. All their challenges and obstacles were successfully overcome for two main reasons – creative actions and extraordinary communication. This allowed great understanding among the Argonauts, and negotiations with unusual and not always friendly people and creatures. We can see how communication makes language alive and functional like wind in the sails.

Talking about past, present, and forthcoming events, people engage their minds and hearts to shape their future. Socialization, which is much needed for maintaining effective relationships and mutual support, is defined by the quality of communication. Picking up facts and impressions from an organization's memory and people's experiences and communications develops shared affection. Communication is necessary to leverage human desires and feelings and to marshal numerous opinions to work for the organization's purposes. Critical factors such as involvement, engagement, and integration can't be developed without effective communication.

Strong culture is defined by a clear language of communication. Thus, professionalism is reflected in simple language. By contrast, negative culture reflects event- or trend-driven or spontaneous meanings and words which tend to change from occasion to occasion. To be a positive force in the organization, language must be very specific, commonly accepted, and constant, changing only as necessary.

Communication is responsible for interaction with the external world, helping the organization to learn about customers' tastes, needs, and desires, and to talk with them about the products and services available. High performing organizations show an advanced level of communication. Effective and purposeful communication is a sign of intelligence that can't be replicated by poorly formed competitors. Having a dynamic nature, communication allows development by talking through processes bolt by bolt, operation by operation, and stage by stage, securing intelligent performance and goal achievement.

ACTIVE DOING, OR PRAXIS

Managing emotions and responsibility encourages the engagement of all members in organizational development, applying new processes and practicing skills and competencies on a perpetual basis. In other words, we are talking about a process of organizational praxis, or with reference to Aristotle, active doing through the employment of skills which are fully enacted and realized.

When talking about positive and negative organizational cultures, we need to consider that praxis, or active doing, can differ in its nature, and not always lead to positive results. Only if a positive culture exists in a company can we talk about good praxis, or eupraxia. In eupraxia, people collaborate together, committing to company goals and being fully engaged in the organization's life. Doing so will secure dynamic development and excellent results for years to come.

If a counterproductive culture has conquered an organization, those without a clear understanding of culture will generally regard it as nothing more than bad luck, or dyspraxia. Such an organization has left behind any attempt to enact change. Any dynamism there once was has long since gone. Its members may look busy, but their hearts and minds are not engaged and the whole organization will continue to drift further and further from its original vision and principles. No organization can continue on this trajectory long before it dies.

Maintaining a positive culture is of paramount importance for an organization's existence and sustainable development. Doing so requires active choices and continued effort on the part of the organization's owners, investors, and managers. These choices include actively putting the organization's values into practice. To avoid this choice is to choose to merely be a victim of happenstance, a prisoner of fortune, or misfortune. Such inaction will be sure to lead to a swift death.

Leaders love talking about synergy, often pointing to results in which one plus one seems to equal three. This cannot be possible with only physical resources. An unseen element is necessary. Praxis, or active doing, is that invisible element responsible for the development of this desired extra value.

REVITALIZATION, OR APOPTOSIS

Thinking about an organization as a living body drives us to consider a peculiar process – apoptosis, the phenomenon of programmed cell death. This process is normal and necessary, allowing for new cells to grow and develop. More than fifty billion cells die in a human body every day. It is a process we do not even notice.

The same process happens in organizations. People come and go; the quality of resources is never exactly the same; processes are never perfect; and market changes play their own serious role in shaping the organization. We cannot stop this phenomenon and should not try to. Just as it is for us, apoptosis is good for an organization. In a positive culture, apoptosis allows for the deleting of damaged, infected, or mutated cells and ensures the effective functioning of the immune system. We all know people who are in excellent physical and mental shape even at a very advanced age because of their strong personalities. Organizations are the same. It is great to work for, or partner with, an organization with a positive culture that remains strong and focused from its inception into old age.

Negative apoptosis, being a property of a strong culture, allows the organization to remain in peak condition. Positive or defective apoptosis is characterized by the uncontrolled proliferation of cells, causing horrible diseases such as atrophy and cancer. Biologists distinguish two pathways in which positive apoptosis can flow — intrinsic and extrinsic. In organizational terms, a number of diseases are accredited to it. We see these diseases taking root in a counterproductive culture.

As soon as people in any given department face a stressful situation, this will cause a reaction down the intrinsic pathway and this organizational cell will inevitably kill itself. With the negative signal spreading around the organization, the extrinsic pathway takes charge and all organizational cells are reprogrammed for death. For instance, employing an increasing number of unprofessional and unethical employees is a precursor to positive apoptosis.

Negative culture management of this kind creates a sense of meaninglessness which leads to a positive apoptosis, triggering the growth of organizational 'parasites' who are like cancer cells, causing the business to suffer further. Unprofessional and unethical people, as aggressive aliens, view a company's culture and use it only for quick personal gain. Such people tend to grow in numbers, slowly killing the company from the inside. An outsider can often detect the resultant atmosphere and will look elsewhere for places to take their business.

SELF-DETECTION, OR HOMEOSTASIS

As soon as we talk about culture as a system which is responsible for the inner organizational environment, we must consider that every system has compulsory properties. A strong system is a composition of well-regulated and productive elements. A faulty or weak system reflects that its inner elements are unbalanced and damaged.

In biological terms, the inner harmony of different roles and functions and other variable elements is regulated by a property known as homeostasis. Homeostasis is a physiological mechanism responsible for detecting deviations in elements not functioning in accordance with assumed standards, deleting damaged cells, and the correction of errors or malfunctioning elements.

A positive culture plays a role similar to homeostasis in an organizational context, regulating inner relations, balancing and stimulating knowledge and information sharing, enhancing competences, and warning against people's misbehavior. For instance, if culture stimulates knowledge sharing then results will be seen in advanced organizational competences. In a counterproductive culture, homeostasis will not function properly, thus organizational competencies will not be developed due to a damaged knowledge and information flow.

Culture is a psychological regulator of the complex inner organizational world. It keeps an organization's communication channels open and stimulating. If damaged due to a negative culture, communications loops become low or broken altogether. Without good communication, no clear understanding or tacit knowledge can be developed amongst employees.

I enjoyed watching the effects of homeostasis on a team in a Starbucks' coffee shop in Birmingham, England, which I visited on a daily basis for a couple of years. My experience was the same every time. People were supportive of each other, flexible in their duties, and treated their jobs with respect, taking responsibility for everything that happened there. I heard a barista talking to a new member of staff about the preferences of the regular customers, and saw the manager professionally solving a conflict with a non-sober customer. The environment in this shop was as warm and enjoyable as the cup of fresh coffee I got there every day; the strong culture of the team demonstrating homeostasis at its best. Needless to say, this location makes plenty of money for its owners along with good memories for customers.

Damaged homeostasis reflects such organizational diseases as cross syndrome, incoordination syndrome, tie atrophy, and stiffness which are discussed in Organisational Anatomy (Konovalov 2016, 150). Organizational metabolism is responsible for the growth of the organization and its responsiveness to the environment and itself is directly dependent on the peculiar role of culture of homeostasis.

Self-Regulating, or Entropy

An effective organization is a fist of concentrated energy contributed by every employee and directed towards the achievement of particular goals, guaranteeing high performance. These individual inputs vary in their quality and value. It is great when all streams of energy are pure and synchronized. However, problems arise when inputs turn negative and are contradictory in nature. Useful energy could be dissipated or simply wasted due to underperforming departments. In practical terms, it means low performance with well-known negative consequences.

Any organization has boundaries, resource limitations, a certain number of people involved, prescribed patterns of processes, and time horizons to produce value in terms of products or service. Quality of resources, expertise, and variations in demand can lead to an enormous number of configurations influencing the result of an organization's activity for better or worse. In real terms, not all employees may act in accordance with assigned roles, and their expertise can be far from adequate to execute a business model successfully. A thoroughly planned business becomes nothing more than a funny computer game for them.

Consistent excellence in production and competitiveness demands teamwork, advanced knowledge, and competences in applying it. A professional and collaborative environment exists only in organizations with a positive culture. Such collaboration will result in the constant improvement of processes. In a negative culture, the organization's elements don't work well and the best they do is to try to fix already broken processes. An organization in this kind of shape will find it very difficult to move from a weak to a strong culture.

How can we understand these inconsistencies and disorders from an organizational culture standpoint? Here, the laws of thermodynamics offer insight, specifically concerning entropy. Entropy is a measure of the number of configurations that a system can have when in a state specified by certain microscopic variables. It often reveals a system's disorders.

Entropy is a function of an intelligent cultural system, one which should be self-regulating. It signals if any energy is wasted which is restricting the company from further development. How does it work? As an example, Special Forces troops demonstrate prominent entropy in their internal culture. They have zero tolerance for an underperforming team member regardless of rank, are famous for superior tactical knowledge, support the weakest and wounded in battle, and everyone performs together toward a common goal. They are masters of collaboration. Those who do not comply with the team's culture are immediately spotted, expelled, and actions are taken to restore the team's performance capacity.

Organizational preparedness for change, flexibility, and endurance are directly associated with entropy which allows a company to withstand challenges. Any organization or state in which culture accommodates entropy can be considered a winner. It can be sure that its own internal culture will generate the best possible solution when problems inevitably arise.

Counterproductive cultures simply lack entropy as a property. They tolerate misbehavior, inconsistencies in processes, and patchy collaboration, all of which destroy a company without mercy. Such a culture does not have an ingrained function of maintaining reliable and flexible systems capable of offering appropriate configurations of expertise, knowledge, and competences when needed.

FOCUS ON PEOPLE

Nineteenth-century German writer Johann Wolfgang von Goethe stated, "The way you see people is the way you treat them, and the way you treat them is what they become." Any organization is a complex living body consisting of members with different personal, intellectual, and psychological qualities. Therefore, each member plays a unique part in an organization's symphony. The issue is that in an orchestra, members can hear each other, enjoying performing and satisfying listeners. In most organizations, this aspect is not always prominent. Again, culture plays the role of a catalyzer responsible for recovering or restoring losses which occur during a transfer of cultural values and meaning from owners and leaders to organizational members.

To a great extent, culture should be considered as a helping hand for people who are adapting to a company environment. If positive and strong, then culture acts as a garden where people's natural qualities and desires are cultivated for their own benefit as well as that of the organization.

Culture is only productive if centered on stimulating people, growing each individual in the process, and helping them to reach the organization's goals; otherwise, it becomes abusive and destructive. In other words, people-centered culture leads to productivity, and the lack thereof, leads to a negative culture of disillusionment. We have all encountered cashiers or service providers who cannot answer our questions or are not willing to satisfy even minor requests, invoking purported company policy. This turns customers, stakeholders, and partners away. I would suggest that these service providers are not happy responding in this way, sounding unprofessional and feeling incapable of helping. Additionally, it fosters little chance for productive relationships and collaboration among employees. People enjoy performing and revealing their best qualities and skills in an environment which allows enhancement of their professional and life experiences with humanistic goals which go beyond mere profit.

As soon as the focus of culture is shifted from people, i.e. employees, customers, and partners, onto something else, such as processing systems or automated customer relationship management, then culture stops being a positive force. Turning attention away from people is like placing a sign on an organization's entrance door which shouts "We disrespect you!"

Positive culture is a reflection of an organization's respect for employees and external stakeholders. People will respect a company that respects them; no one will respect a company that does not respect them. As a result, people will not give their best effort as employees or patronize such a company as customers. In simple words, if employees feel respected and appreciated they become more productive, more loyal, more obliged to work effectively, and more engaged in company life.

GAIN OR LOSE

Let's imagine that you have bought a very advanced gadget at a hefty price. Then you use it only as a fancy accessory, ignoring the practical use that you paid top dollar for. With time, many of the features become outdated and the device loses its appeal.

A similar scenario often happens in businesses where managers are not fully realizing the role of culture. As a result, the most powerful means of mass inspiration, encouragement, and company enrichment is not appropriately exploited. These managers seem to mistakenly assume that because culture does not have a price tag like a piece of software or company car, then it is not a valuable investment of time and resources, and will take care of itself, which is a drastically mistaken point of view.

Culture is intangible, but valuable and critical in terms of the company's existence and success. Yet, it can't be analyzed using first-order logic as it contains too many variables, and, therefore, is not simply something to manage. The complexity of culture makes people suspicious and skeptical, as they are not usually prepared to shift the dimensions and patterns of their thinking. However, complexity is merely a pack of simple items which are manageable if divided into digestible parts and elements.

This demands a view from other angles. The reason for discussing the functions of organizational culture as critical properties in such a manner is to offer a sophisticated view, allowing leaders to gain a superior understanding of the very nature of culture as its metaphysical nature often remains invisible to leaders and those still climbing the ladder. It is difficult to manage culture without an intimate understanding of its properties and functions.

If you desire to strengthen your business by adding strategic value, unique competitive advantage, and extra capacity, then taking care of organizational culture is a starting point on this journey to success.

Corporate Superpower details
http://wbp.bz/CSpower

Printed in Great Britain
by Amazon